LOVE IS MY RELIGION

VOLUME 3

LOVE IS MY RELIGION

VOLUME 3

MATA AMRITANANDAMAYI
COMPILED BY JANINE CANAN MD

Love Is My Religion by Mata Amritanandamayi
compiled by Janine Canan MD
Copyright © 2020 by Mata Amritanandamayi Center
All rights reserved.
Except for the Introduction by Janine Canan, or for brief review,
no portion of this book may be reproduced, stored in a retrieval system,
transmitted in any form or by any means, or translated into any language,
without the written permission of the publisher.

Quotations in this book have been compiled from books, pamphlets, magazines,
films and songs published by Mata Amritanandamayi Math, India,
and Mata Amritanandamayi Center, USA;
from the web site www.Amritapuri.org, Amma's public talks and comments,
interviews and remarks to the editor.

Published by Mata Amritanandamayi Center
P.O. Box 613, San Ramon, California 95483
United States of America
www.amma.org
www.theammashop.org

First Printing: March 2020

ISBN-13: 978-1-68037-871-9

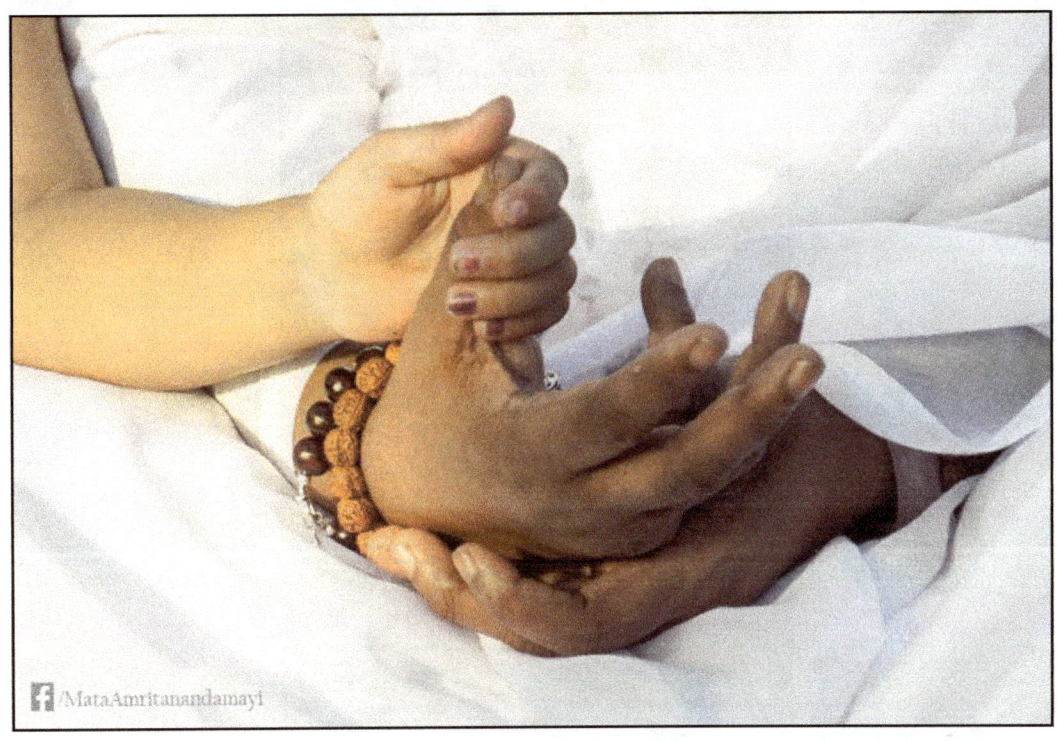

CONTENTS

16. A Guiding Light — 8

17. The Disciple — 62

18. Realization — 94

19. Supreme Self — 128

20. The Flower — 164

21. Faith — 180

22. The Beauty of Life — 216

23. This Moment — 228

24. Pure Love — 246

*Photographs of Sri Mata Amritanandamayi
cover, title page, 5 & 6*

16
A GUIDING LIGHT

If you are saving God for the day
all your problems are solved and your mind is at peace,
you are making a grave mistake —
that day will never come.

At any moment we can lose our health or our mind
and then we will have lived in vain.
The time to set off on the road to our true Self is now.

Most people view life as a struggle for survival and settle
for an adequate job, income, home, spouse and children.

But we have a higher purpose: To know and realize who we are!

The purpose of life is to experience what lies beyond our physical existence.

We will never find fulfillment if we do not direct our energy
toward the supreme goal of life.

Our responsibilities in the world should help us fulfill our higher responsibility
to become aware of our oneness with the universal Soul.

Planning to lead a spiritual life after fulfilling all our desires
is like standing at the seashore waiting for all the waves to stop before going in.

It is pointless to try to satisfy all our desires before embarking on our journey.
Desires are as endless as the ocean waves—they will never cease.

There is a Krishna, a Buddha or a Christ within each of us.

The capacity for enlightenment lies dormant in everyone—
even those who are selfish and cruel.

Our selfishness springs from our identification with the ego—the sense of I and mine.
Convinced that we are limited and incomplete, we struggle
for what we think we need to be happy.
In Reality we are eternal, blissful and complete.

God is definitely inside us.
We are treasure chests full of diamonds,
but out of ignorance we keep searching for the diamonds outside us.

The amount of happiness we derive from external things is a mere fraction
of the happiness each of us carries inside.

Happiness is within us, but our likes and dislikes
prevent us from experiencing it.

Because we are controlled by the ego, we cling to them anyway.
To break free, we require the guidance of an authentic spiritual master.

To realize the true Self, the ego and its tendencies,
attractions and aversions must be eliminated.
To accomplish this, we need a master who dwells in pure Consciousness.

Only a spiritual master whose inner Eye is open, can really help us heal.
An ordinary person, with ordinary eyes, cannot do it.

In a true master we see our joy and our suffering reflected.
Neither happy nor sad, the master mirrors us.
A clouded ego cannot reflect another's feelings—
it is blind and only sees itself.

An imperfect person cannot remove the imperfections of another.
Only those who have studied can teach; only those who have acquired can give.

Only those who have conquered sorrow can free us from sorrow
and bestow lasting happiness and peace.

To help someone overcome pain, heal and change,
one needs to be at a higher level of Consciousness.
Anyone who seeks spiritual wisdom, requires a master who has studied,
practiced and experienced the Truth.

What matters most in a spiritual teacher is the level of his or her Consciousness.
A fully realized Soul has reached the supreme peak.

To get a human body is exceedingly difficult.
But it is even more difficult to get a human life inclined toward spirituality.
Most difficult and rare by far is a life lived
in the company of a perfect master.

To uncover our hidden godly gifts, we require a master
who knows the supreme Reality.

A true guru is a reservoir of God—of divine Light.

A true guru kindles the light of Knowledge and dispels the darkness of ignorance.

Knowledge, the real teacher, comes in a human form.

Only one who has realized the Truth, can lead us to the goal.
Only one who has realized the Self, can give us the right advice at the right time.

Only a realized guru can lead us back to our true Self and Source.

Once we come to a fully realized guru, our inner development can advance
and we can start maturing into our Supreme Self.

We need an atmosphere conducive to spiritual growth
and the guru's presence offers the ideal climate.
The guru knows the supreme Reality—all we have to do
is place ourselves in their presence and accept their guidance.

The guru experiences Reality and by association we can rapidly connect with it.

We have to grow into our true nature gradually.
A master who can perceive and correct our weaknesses helps us to grow.

Although ultimately the guru is internal,
we need an outer guru until our inner guru awakens.

Guru and God are in everything.
But we need the outer guru until we can perceive
the essential Truth in everything on our own.
Once we reach that point, the whole universe becomes our guru.

Those who have the unshakeable faith to see in every situation, whether good or bad,
a message from God, need no outer guru — but how many souls
really have that kind of strength and resolve?

A true guru is like an express bus that will take us to our destination faster.

When we go on a journey and rely on a map, we do not know the road conditions—
the state of repair, the presence of wild animals or robbers.
But if we travel with a trustworthy companion who knows the way,
we can travel with confidence.

The road to liberation is a maze of intricate paths—a labyrinth.
In traveling through the maze, a spiritual aspirant may not be able to figure out
where to go or which way to turn.

The guru knows all there is to know—
knows that what you see and hear are merely illusions.
The guru makes this clear, so you do not get trapped into believing
that what you perceive is reality.
The guru constantly encourages and inspires you to go further and further—
beyond the jungles of illusion—until you eventually arrive
at the shore of enlightenment.

Remember, the path that leads to the state of realization is very narrow.
Two people cannot walk it hand in hand, rubbing shoulders—we have to walk it alone.
As we walk the path, a light is guiding us—the light of the guru's grace.
The guru walks before us, shedding light on our path, slowly and carefully leading us.
The guru knows all the intricate paths by heart.
The light of her grace helps us to see and remove the obstacles
and reach the ultimate goal.

A true master can take us from the state of a beggar
to that of emperor of the Universe—
from the state of a receiver to that of a true benefactor.

The guru comes to the seeker—we do not need to go searching!
But first we have to release our grip on the world.

To know our true nature we have to turn our gaze inward.
We are constantly thinking about external matters, other people and things.
We have to look inward and face our weaknesses.

Anger and jealousy are weaknesses.
Hatred, selfishness and fear are all weaknesses.
And their root cause is the ego.

The ego is illusory and has no independent existence.
It only seems real because of the animating power of pure Being.
Without that power the ego is lifeless and inert.
If we do not support it, it withdraws and disappears.

Though the perceptions of the ego have no real power, they mislead us
and turn us away from our real nature and master —
which is our soul and true Self.

A false master controls, misleads and deludes us — blocking the face of Reality.
We need to break out of our constricting mental shell!
Once it cracks and drops away, the seedling will sprout,
rise and grow into a fully mature tree.

The seed and the tree are both real
but the tree has realized its potential and the seed has not.
A tree produces food, shade, shelter and other benefits, which a seed cannot do.
Once we develop to our full capacity, we will be able to benefit the world.

To eliminate the ego, we need the master's guidance.

The master teaches us to go within and deal with our own deficiencies.

The master would like to take us to the goal as soon as possible
but first the ego must be released — the shell broken.

To know the Truth we have to let go of I-ness and my-ness.
This is very difficult to do when we practice on our own.

Meditation is very important for attaining peace, prosperity and freedom,
but has to be practiced carefully under the supervision of a master.

Spiritual growth depends on the mind and body—it is crucial
not to damage either by careless practices!

Practicing spirituality by following book instructions is dangerous.
Scriptural study and spiritual practice are two different things—
one is theory, the other is practice.
We need the supervision of a teacher in order to learn how to practice correctly.

Practicing on your own may increase your powers, but to realize the Self
you must surrender to a realized master.

What distinguishes a true Teacher from an imposter?
Around an enlightened Soul immersed in God there shines
a palpable aura of Love and peace, untainted by any ego or selfishness.

A truly realized Soul opens her arms to everyone and out of profound awareness
of inner equality, treats everyone equally
regardless of their age, class, wealth, race or religion.

True masters do not criticize or blame others.
Peace and tranquility are their very nature.
Anger cannot overpower them.
Any show of anger is for the sole purpose
of correcting and guiding humanity—
it is an expression of their Love.

While we constantly need to renounce our negativities,
a master's heart has zero tolerance for them
and they are compelled to renounce the master.

A true master places no importance on extrasensory powers or siddhis.
Already in possession of all the power he or she needs,
a real master is simple and humble.

Simplicity and humility are the essential qualities of a great Soul.

**Through their humility and service realized Souls set an example
they hope will be emulated by the world.**

**Humility follows on the dawn of Knowledge.
When we truly know, we are humble.
When we perceive pure Consciousness in everyone,
we feel respect for everyone.**

**True masters bow down to the divine Light, which they see everywhere.
When we see everything as divine, we are spontaneously worshipful.
All otherness vanishes and life becomes an act of worship,
a prayer and a song of praise.
When we perceive enlightenment, the inmost Self, latent in everything,
we can only feel profound reverence.
Nothing is insignificant—everything has a special place.
Every blade of grass is dazzling.**

As a master sculptor views a block of stone—
looking past its rough exterior to behold the beautiful form hidden inside—
a spiritual master beholds the true Self hidden in all things.

A pure master can see through the walls of the individual ego
to the hidden Light waiting to burst forth.

When we are drawn to someone whom we believe to be a true master,
it is important to use our power of discrimination.
If we are not fully enlightened, our intuition is not yet fully integrated
into our higher Self, and our feelings cannot be entirely trusted.
Mesmerized by certain powers, we easily imagine we have found what we seek.

It is not surprising that certain self-seeking individuals have pretended
to be enlightened and taken advantage of the human thirst for spiritual guidance.
The West has suffered a great deal from this
and consequently developed paranoia toward gurus in general.

Because of a few charlatans, we should not lose faith that authentic masters exist.
Would we let quacks keep us from going to a doctor when we are sick?

To lead a disciple from bondage to freedom, a master
must be totally free of egoistic tendencies and mental attachments.
How can a master bound to his personal whims and fancies possibly free anyone?

In a real master there is not a trace of desire.
Desire arises from the mind and when the mind dissolves, desire dissolves entirely.
So-called gurus who exploit their disciples sexually, or in any way
try to force their will on others, are not genuine — far from it!
They are still strongly identified with their own desires.

A true spiritual master has gone beyond the mind and ego.
Sexual energy has been converted into pure vital energy
and is used entirely for the good of the world.

A real master has progressed from the lowest sexual center or chakra
to the highest center of human existence, the crown chakra
of Truth, Consciousness and Bliss.

The body moves but Consciousness is unmoving.

The true guru is beyond the body and beyond the human.
A Satguru is an incarnation of pure nameless, formless Consciousness.
No individuality exists, only nothingness.
How could the Formless and Nameless ever take from us or control us?
A true guru simply is, and we are the recipients of the blessing of their presence.

One with Existence, a great Soul is indebted to no one.
The life of such a Soul is perfect and complete as it is.
It simply exists as divine Presence.
Can boundless space, the Sun, the wind or the ocean ever be in debt?
What could a great master possibly ever want from us?
It is we who owe everything to the master.

Everything a realized Soul does, sends a message of life's deepest Truth.
Every word and gesture is intended to awaken the human soul.

Like iron filings drawn to a powerful magnet, we cannot resist
the spontaneous Love and attraction we experience
when we approach a truly great master.

Wherever great Souls appear, people gather round—attracted like dust to a whirlwind.
Their breath, even the breeze that touches their body, benefits the world.

The guru is a living experience beyond logic, judgment or intellect.

Genuine seekers experience an awakening of the heart
in the presence of a genuine master of Truth.

The Sun does not do anything in particular to make a lotus bloom.
It simply shines in the sky, and because it exists
all the lotuses on Earth effortlessly open.
The presence of a perfect master is like a radiant Sun
that makes the Heart Lotus blossom—there is no question of force.
Such a master's infinitely loving and compassionate presence has the power
to melt the rock of the ego and create a flow of supreme Love.

In the presence of a truly great master, the closed heart opens up
and we become as receptive, innocent and obedient as a little child.

A great master steals our hearts and souls and fills them with pure and innocent Love.

Although we cannot see the wind, we can feel it.
The grandeur of a genuine master is felt by the heart.

A genuine master is never discovered by mind games—only by a pure heart.

We recognize a real master because she, or he, is nothing but our own true Self.

What attracts the master to the seeker and awakens the inner truth
is the seeker's Love, devotion and faith.

The master does not teach and yet, without being taught, we learn.
The master's presence, her life, is the great Lesson.
Transformation happens effortlessly and uncontrollably.

Only Love can create this miracle.

A perfect master lives in the world with the selfless intent of leading humanity
out of the darkness, and is constantly setting an example for us to follow.
As the living Truth, a great master embodies the holiest of qualities —
Love, purity, sacrifice, patience and forgiveness.

A great Soul would never do anything to hurt anyone
because they know that everything is One.

True gurus have no selfish interest.
Their lives and being are renunciation itself.
Their bodies burn with renunciation to uplift their disciples
and benefit the entire world.

From their blazing flames we light our wicks
and shine our lights on the dark road that humanity has chosen.

It takes endless patience to guide disciples
with all their weaknesses and negative tendencies.
Sacrifice and austerity are eternally ablaze in the life of a true guru.

Of all the austerities ever practiced, patience is the supreme austerity.

All we need to do, is live in the guru's presence and try to receive
and absorb their sacrifice into our lives.

Pure Love is formless—
only when It flows through a living being
can It be perceived with our senses.

Love cannot be taught, but in the presence of a supreme master
we can feel and gradually develop it.

A flower needs no instruction to blossom;
a nightingale no music teacher to sing.
What happens is unforced and spontaneous.
In the presence of a heart perpetually overflowing with Love
the human heart blossoms naturally.

In the presence of Love, our thoughts spontaneously subside
and our hearts spread open their lovely fragrant petals.

Love simply happens!
Suddenly an irresistible overwhelming longing for Oneness
gushes forth from the heart.

Release all your sorrow, my darling children,
and merge in the sacred OM.
You are the I in me, and I am the you in you.
The sense of any difference is only due to blind ignorance.
In reality, there is no separation—nothing is separate.

Pure Love transcends the body and exists between hearts.
For Love there is no barrier or boundary.
The lotus blossoms no matter how far from the Sun.
For Love there is no distance.

Child, you and Mother are not two—we are one.
There is no I or you—only Love.

We speak of God and devotee, master and disciple,
but only Love can impart the knowledge of Oneness,
the all-encompassing reality of the Soul.

Without the passport of Love, we will never be given the visa for Freedom.

Open the door of your heart and discover that it was never locked.
Whatever you thought — it was always open!

Spread your wings and limbs and move beyond your body and mind into Space.
Leave the boundaries behind you and enjoy the bliss of eternal freedom.

Children, your biological mother will tend to your needs in this lifetime
(even this is rare nowadays), but Amma will guide you
to Bliss in all your lives to come.

Do not think of Amma as only this body.
When you pray sincerely, the vibrations reflect on her mind.
Their pure innocent intent draws Her to you
and you can feel her presence and experience peace.

Everyone has a direct hotline to Mother.
The quality of the connection depends upon the fervor of your call.

Just as a mountain climber always has a lifeline,
Mother is always present, even in the most dangerous of situations.
Allow Her to take your hand.

Knowledge cannot be forced — only conveyed to
and stimulated in one who is receptive.
If your nose is stuffy, you cannot enjoy the flower's perfume
and there is no point in blaming the flower.

Only if you unlock the door, can the master enter.

We need to approach the master with an open heart
if we wish to understand her meaning.

Without Love, surrender, knowledge and effort
we cannot reach the ultimate goal
and fulfill the purpose of life.

As a seed surrenders by sinking into the dirt in order to become a mature tree,
we must surrender to Existence in total humility in order to become our true Self.

Once we realize that God is all pervading, all powerful, all knowing
and purer than the purest, our consciousness
naturally fills with reverence and awe.

Spiritual understanding requires the humility of a beginner.

To gather the seeds of knowledge we must bow down.

Humility helps us to surrender.

Once we can be humble and patient and surrender,
the master will reach out.

As we increasingly surrender to the master,
our world-view will change and distortions in our perceptions disappear.

Freedom does not mean that the world disappears—
but that our mistaken notions about it disappear.

The guru shows us the wounds festering inside us,
their potential for damaging, even ruining our lives,
and how they can heal—with the boundless Love and compassion of the guru.

A true master teaches us to accept everything that happens in life—
to be thankful for both good and bad, right and wrong, friend and enemy,
those who harm and those who help us, those who imprison and those who set us free.

The master helps us forget the dark past
and the bright future full of a thousand promises
and live in the fullness of the present moment—recognizing that all of Nature,
everyone and everything, even our enemy is helping us evolve to perfection.

Every human being is destined to pass through both good and bad experiences,
but when we follow the instructions of a perfect master,
we emerge from our ordeals unscathed.

Once we have opened, we discover that the Sun was always shining
and the wind was always carrying Love's sweet scent.
No special conditions, no force were needed.

To prevent infection and support the healing of a wound
we clean it first and then apply the medicine.
To further our spiritual growth we should clean the ego with devotional practices
to prepare us for sacred Knowledge.

As the ironsmith melts the rod before hammering it into shape,
we should melt the heart with Love before shaping it with Knowledge.

If we cultivate the attitude of a servant toward all,
our hearts will become all-accommodating
and divine grace will automatically pour in.

We cannot reach Reality with even a speck of selfishness.

The ego is only eliminated by the conviction that I am everyone's servant.
Only with this attitude can we ever know God.

The pinnacle of devotion is perfect Love.

As our consciousness expands, the sense of mine—
my mother, my father, my child, my family—will recede
and everything will become Yours.

Today, the best path for most people is the path of Devotion or Bhakti—
which means learning to see everything as pervaded by God.

Bhakti, the path of heart and devotion, is the easiest path for our age
and bears fruit from the outset.

We should begin by saying, "I am your servant"—
and later on when we can patiently take a beating, we can say, "I am God."

We cannot experience Atman, the supreme Soul, simply by reading the scriptures.
Scriptures are a map easily misunderstood and frequently misleading.
Vedanta study more often inflates than deflates the ego.

There is no point in walking around saying "I am God"
when we are just starting out on the path.

The egg has to lie under the mother hen and incubate before it can hatch.
A seeker has to practice under the guidance of a guru.
Sitting around proclaiming "I am God" does not help.
Would we say "I am a hen, if we were an egg?

Through surrender we seek freedom from worldly ties, dissolution of the mind,
transcendence of the body and intellect, and ultimately,
through the guru's discipline and grace,
Self-realization and freedom.

Once we can bow down, real growth can begin.

As water flows downhill, the grace of the guru naturally pours into the humble.

A humble attitude—awareness and acceptance of our ignorance—
creates the receptivity and openness required for the master to pour in pure Knowledge.

A thick rough thread only passes through the eye of the needle
when thin and smooth enough to be able to bend and enter the narrow passage.
Only then, can it stitch the cloth together.
Similar surrender is necessary to enter the supreme Reality.

We have to cultivate the quality of surrender.

In the presence of a true master,
we need to completely accept our ignorance and surrender.

Spiritual understanding requires the humility of a beginner.
To gather the seeds of Knowledge, we need to bow down.

Without humility, spiritual growth is impossible.

Only with the sword of humility can we chop off the head of the ego.

Like drainage water full of impurities and toxins, we need to be purified.
As we pass through the various processes of purification,
we exhaust both obvious and hidden impurities.
This can be quite painful and could cause a skeptic to conclude that God does not exist.
But this very struggle and suffering speeds up our cleansing,
dissolving old karmic bondages.

We possess the key to the treasure chest,
but it is rusty and needs to be cleaned and polished.
To know God, the ego has to be removed—that is why we have come to the guru.
Now it is time to surrender and humbly obey.

When we fly on an airplane we are told to fasten the seat belt
for our own safety—not to dominate us.
The guru asks us to obey certain rules and practice certain restraints
both to uplift us and to protect us from the dangerous impulses of the ego.

Great masters teach us to respond consciously and not react reflexively.
Their lives are living monuments to this great principle of life.

To build a tower that rises high into the sky,
a solid foundation must first be poured into the ground.
To rise we need humility.
True power is grounded in true respect.

What if a seed puffed itself up and proclaimed,
"I do not want to bow down and grovel in the dirt—I am a tree!"
A seed contains a tree, but if it stays in the storeroom it will be devoured by the mice.
Only when a seed goes into the earth can its mature form emerge.
To grow tall and bear fruit, it has to get into the dirt.

The only way to uproot the ego is to bow your head.
To eventually bear fruit, the seed must bow to the Earth and allow itself to be submerged.

The presence of a realized guru provides the most favorable climate
for the seed of divinity to sprout.
It offers abundant opportunities for our growth,
but it is we who must seize them.

We are the absolute Self, but it is not enough to just say this!
We have to experience it.

Experience is the real Guru.

Until we realize that we are helpless
and the ego cannot save us—that nothing belongs to us—
God or the guru will continue to create circumstances to help us realize this.

We have to do more than use our God-given faculties and talents to follow our whims.
If we have chosen the path of spirituality,
we should not sit around waiting for divine grace.

Realization does not come automatically—there is great work to be done!
It cannot be bought and does not materialize out of thin air.

Evolution is slow for devotees who want to keep
their attachments, possessions, reputation and fame.
Living in luxury, indulging in the pleasures of life, deepens our habits
and lengthens the karmic chain—the distance to be traveled back to our Source.

Sincere devotees and disciples will arrive at the Source sooner.

We can reach perfection rapidly if we truly commit ourselves to the ultimate goal.

God, guru and grace are always present.
We have the capacity and faculties to experience and to know them.
The master provides the map and directions through their words.
The winds of Grace are forever blowing.
The holy River is ever flowing, the Sun of Knowledge ever shining.
And finally the master's work is done.

The principle of the Guru is eternal.
When we are close to the guru our divine Power awakens.
Our spiritual practices nourish it and it flourishes.
The guru's Presence brings out our virtues and our practices bear fruit.
And one day we discover that the senses that once enslaved us, now serve us.

The guru is the door that leads from bondage to freedom.

Established in a permanent state of Bliss—
perfect, complete, beyond which there is nothing more—
the guru is expansive as the sky, vast as the ocean,
invisible as the wind and continuous as a river.
The guru is pure Presence and has no sense of being the guru.
As the wind, the sky and the ocean make no claims
and have nothing to prove, since the proof is inherent in their very being,
the guru's majesty resides in the incomparability,
the indestructibility and the infinity of absolute Being.

Like Eternity, the principle of the Guru is ineffable and indescribable.
The guru is a manifestation of the whole universe in a human form.
The greatness of the guru can only be experienced by the heart.
As the guru's infinite Energy comes streaming toward us,
we spontaneously blossom into Love, faith, devotion and surrender.

Self-realization is the end of suffering and the ultimate goal of life.
If the effort is made, realization can happen.
If we have a living master and strive for the master's grace,
Self-realization will occur.

To receive grace we must be humble — not just bow down but express our Love.
Children, may your heartfelt, selfless Love for Supreme Being illuminate the world.

We cannot know when Grace may come — we can only wait.
The time and place are chosen by God and the guru.
When the time is ripe, it suddenly happens —
we become a fully conscious, innocent child.

Children, blessings and grace are at the disposal of the master
and bestowed when she or he desires.
Grace is a strange phenomenon—
when, where, how it occurs cannot be predicted.
If the master desires, the blessing of Self-realization can be granted instantly—
even to a stranger who has performed no spiritual practices—
or can be denied to a long-time, dedicated practitioner.
A great Soul can fulfill a life-long desire for no reason whatsoever.

God is like a little child with no interest in proud ascetics
who sometimes showers grace on innocents
who have done nothing to deserve it.

To receive grace we should cry,
pray and cling to the guru's feet,
no matter what.

To make the best use of your guru, surrender to your own true Self—
for your Self and the guru's Self are one and the same.

In the presence of a Great Soul, we can experience Love,
compassion, self-sacrifice and other divine qualities.
But it is as if we stood viewing a vast ocean from the shore.
We can only see an infinitesimal portion of its immensity—
just enough to realize that it is beyond measure.
We cannot penetrate its depths—only by diving in can we do that.
Our own Self is just as vast and deep.

To jump in, is to truly surrender.
And this takes enormous courage—
for it means the death of the body and the mind.

To plunge into the Ocean takes courage, surrender and a great sense of adventure!

The mind includes the ego, the sense of I,
and this is the cause of all our self-centeredness.
We have to discover our real center in the Self—Existence itself—
and release our individual mind and ego.

To surrender takes very great courage—the courage to give up yourself
and accept and welcome everything, without sorrow or regret.
To sacrifice the ego takes bravery—indeed, real daring.

Surrendering to a master is not easy—it takes tremendous courage!
It is like jumping into a river whose current will inexorably carry you to the ocean.
Once you jump in, there is no escape.
You can put up a fight and try to swim against the colossal current, but it is useless.
You are on your way to the Ocean of Being—your true home.

We can choose to stay on the shore or dive in—
but once we take the leap, we are powerless as a corpse.

We no longer have any choice—we can only be still
and let the current take us where it will.
We have to surrender our individuality and dissolve.
And ultimately, we will find ourselves floating in pure Consciousness.

When we surrender to higher Consciousness, we surrender all our claims
and release our grip on everything we were holding onto.
Loss and gain lose all their meaning.
We no longer want to be something—we want to be nothing, absolutely nothing.
And so we plunge into the river of Existence.

Swimming on the surface is pleasant,
but diving into the ocean is a huge, utterly different kind of adventure
in an unknown world of Mystery.
Diving into the ocean is difficult—
we have to hold our breath, bend over and submerge.
But once we surrender, the ocean's hidden treasures are revealed to us.
And the deeper we go, the more we see and realize, the more we thirst to know—
until finally we can touch the very ground of Being.

We may not take the plunge now—we may not be ready
to jump into the river's fathomless depths.
We may prefer to keep standing on the bank basking in its beauty,
its soft cool breeze and powerful babbling magic.
The river will not force us—we can stay as long as we wish.
It will not send us away saying, "Enough, go, a long line is waiting."
Nor will it insist, "Now is the time, either jump or I will make you."
It is entirely up to us individually—the river is always ready
and waiting to accept and cleanse us.

We are free to simply stand on the shore, but how long will we stay?
Sooner or later we will turn back to the world or jump in.
And if we return to the world, the beauty and enchantment of the river
will keep luring us back until one day, tempted to take the leap,
we will finally, inevitably dive in.

Humanity is evolving into God.
Every human being is essentially divine.

Evolution from the human to the divine is a slow process
involving an enormous amount of carving, molding, remolding and polishing.
It takes immense work and patience and cannot be done in a hurry.
Revolution may be fast, but it kills and destroys.

Spiritual growth is evolutionary, not revolutionary.
In our impatience, humans tend to be revolutionary.
But revolution is always destructive.
Unfortunately, in the modern age people want spiritual expansion
as fast as possible—we want instant enlightenment.
Can you imagine a mother saying to her baby, "I want you to grow up right now.
Why are you still a child? Hurry up, I can't wait any longer!"
What would we say about such a mother except that she is either very foolish or mad.
We expect a miracle and lack the patience to wait and make an effort.
We do not understand that the real miracle is the opening of the heart
into the supreme Truth—an inner blossoming that is always slow and steady.

Everything in Nature is evolutionary.

God takes great care and is extremely patient
even with the opening of a flower, which is a miracle.
It takes a child nine months to be ready for birth — another miracle.
God never hurries — God evolves.
Real growth happens only when we are evolutionary.

With humility, patience and surrender,
we can find an excellent guide to show us the Way.
God in the form of the guru will take the disciple by the hand,
and through obedience and surrender we will eventually reach the final Goal.

If we are able to surrender, we will be blessed with victory.

The Light of the guru's grace will enable us to see and surmount
every obstacle on the path.

When we follow the master's instructions they will bear fruit —
this is a debt the master must repay.

Love is the essence of every human being—Love and joy are hidden in each of us.
When Love touches and awakens our goodness, we often shed tears.
Mother is a catalyst.
Her embrace is not merely physical—it touches the soul.

Everyone is Amma's child.
All are received and none are refused.
All are given the same opportunity, the same Love, the same darshan.
How we experience it, depends on our receptivity.
Darshan is a never-ending continuous flow that only needs to be received.

The more we open in darshan, the more we can receive.
If we can momentarily abandon the mind altogether, we can experience it fully.
Everyone receives at least a glimpse of who we truly are.
In Amma and in you, there is only one Reality—
the blissful silence of Love.

Seeing the divine Mother in you,
Amma bows down to her own Self—to God.

You are all my God.
Amma does not have a God who dwells beyond the sky.

Amma is alone when by herself and even in a crowd
because we are all just one.

Child, you and Mother are not two but one.
There is no you or I—there is only Love.

Amma loves everything.
She used to try to embrace the breeze.
When the rains came, She would sing and dance in bliss.
She would gaze and commune with the sky,
talk to the birds, hug and kiss the trees.

There has never been a moment when Mother did not experience
her oneness with the Supreme Power.
At birth, Mother knew there was nothing but God.

Amma is simply an offering to the world.
Her only wish is to be available to all—to give and give and give.

Amma is the servant of all—she lives only in your heart.

As long as her hands can move,
Mother will continue to give darshan.

Amma considers everyone in the world her child.
No one is different from Her.
What She does, She does for her Self.

When you are rooted in the Self, you are always in a giving mood.
You do not feel bored—you constantly want to give.
You do not want anything from anyone.
Mother just wants to give.
She does not need or expect anything.
She accepts everything that happens in her life.

Amma's only wealth is the happiness and welfare of her children.

When her children are happy, Mother is happy.
When her children are sad, Mother is sad.

Amma is like a mother who attends to many other tasks
while simultaneously tending to her child.

Darling children,
Mother does not insist on anything.

It is her joy to see her children moving with mutual support and Love
toward eternal Bliss.

Praying that her children's hearts will fill to the brim and overflow with divine Love,
Amma offers herself to pure Being.

Never forget that you are not alone on this journey.
Mother is always with you—let Her take your hand.

Call Amma.

Whatever you do, never forget the goal of realizing your Soul.
Always remember your goal.

You already are Mother—you simply need to remove
the unnecessary layers obscuring this truth.

Mother is already within you — nearer than the nearest —
the jewel in the lotus of your heart.

There is a predestined time for every individual to come to Mother.

Do not worry, you have come to Mother and now it is her responsibility
to take care of you and make you perfect.

Protection of the devotee is the duty of God.
Protection of the disciple is the duty of the guru — a duty she fulfills
in many different ways and guises.

Love has many, many faces.

At the right time the master will bestow the fruit of your actions.
Because you can only see a small portion of your life,
you are not in a position to evaluate it.

Always remember, this life is only an infinitesimal portion of your total life.

All those with Amma in this lifetime
have been with Her in past lifetimes — although we cannot remember it.

All Mother's children have always been with Her.
There is no such thing as "before meeting Amma".
You met Her a long time ago and have always been under her protection.
Having previously followed her instructions, you are now experiencing her divine grace.

May all of Amma's children be blessed with Awareness.
May all of you find your inner strength and be blessed with divine grace.
To the Supreme Being, Amma offers this.

Trillions of lights can be lit from a flame.
May Amma's children spread the purity of Love everywhere
through kind words and actions, and so may their consciousness expand
and may they progress on their journey to perfection.

Children, Mother is always with you.
When you think of Her, She sees your faces clearly.
Every night lying down in her ashram in India,
She travels all over the world to her children.

Mother is within you and you are within Her.
Every day try to remember Her, sincerely and intensely.

Amma's children are her baby swans.
Like a mother Amma watches over all of you and gathers up any who have strayed.
You are her fledglings and are always safe beneath her wings.

A true guru is like a mother who takes us back to the state of a child—
back to our true innocence.
The whole purpose of a guru is to awaken the slumbering child.

Your innocent mind is Amma's favorite flower.

**Darling Child, you are not alone.
Mother is always with you.**

17

THE DISCIPLE

For Amma, the relationship between the guru and the disciple
is the ultimate relationship and beyond compare.

There are many kinds of relationships in this world,
but the guru-disciple relationship surpasses them as the only bond of Love
that transcends time and destruction
and is free of worldly bondage.

The relationship between guru and disciple is actually
a conversation between the individual self and the supreme Soul.

Faith in the guru is really faith in our own true Self.

To hear and obey our divine inner guidance
we need a disciple's mind.
We need to be able to follow with Love, faith, devotion and discrimination.
Once we possess this mentality God will appear
in the form of a guru to guide us.

It is our intense thirst for the Truth that awakens our inner disciple.

In former times it was the disciple who sought the guru—
but in today's world the guru comes to the disciple.

The guru comes when we are ready.

It is the disciple's love that awakens the guru in the master,
that attracts the guru and activates their special powers.

The qualifications for discipleship are discrimination, detachment, equanimity,
self-discipline, renunciation of desires, and longing for liberation
with the guru's grace—the ocean of compassion
that blesses the disciple with virtue.

While we may increase our mental strength by doing spiritual practices alone,
to realize the true Self we have to become the disciple of a realized Master.

In the dark materialistic age of the Kali Yuga, the world is like a tempting supermarket.
The disciple has to cultivate detachment to transcend the many temptations.
This demands great faith and determination.

The Supreme Self comes in the form of the Master,
but the disciple's surrender and obedience is what will finally take him to the goal.
Surrender awakens our Consciousness, alters our perspective,
and reveals to us a new world.

To reach the highest Truth, the disciple shows reverence and obedience,
which allows him or her to ascend to a higher, more expansive plane
and eventually reach the Truth embodied by the Master.

When we bow to the guru, we are not bowing to an individual
but to the ideal that is embodied by the guru.
We bow to a level of attainment that we desire to attain.

When we surrender to a perfect Master, we are surrendering to Existence itself.

Discipleship is surrender.

Discipleship is certainly not slavery
but the willingness to receive.

For real discipleship to be born, the disciple must learn humility.
Until then, the Master cannot really enter the disciple's life.

Water poured into a full glass cannot penetrate—it spills out.
As long as we are full of ego, God cannot enter.

Only if we open the door, can the guru enter.
Only if we have the attitude of a disciple, can the light of Knowledge
expel the darkness of ignorance.

The vision of the disciple is gross—the vision of the Master is subtle.
Like a doctor who recognizes an illness unknown to the patient,
the master sees things unknown to the disciple.
Only when the disciple becomes aware of his ignorance
will he be able to grow.

The guru guides the disciple out of pure compassion.

To allow the Master to work on us,
we should maintain the attitude that I am nothing.

How can anything be added to a glass that is already full?
Surrender your ego, empty your heart and allow the grace to flow in.

To really be aware, humble and enthusiastic,
disciples must understand that they know nothing!
Only then can they understand the master
and accept and absorb the teachings.

In order to grow, disciples need to understand that the guru
knows their minds better than they do — and this requires trust.

When the storm comes and huge waves heave and swell,
only an experienced captain can save the ship.
Know and stand firm in the conviction that only the master can help you.
Upon this knowledge depends your final victory.

Nothing is more important than the grace of a perfect guru.

Without their loving care, compassionate glance and affectionate touch
we cannot reach the goal.
With them the guru is sending her grace.
Children, pray for her grace.

When we take refuge in the guru,
the power of the guru's austerity and energy flows into us.

Trust in a perfect Master makes it possible for us to shed our ego
and egocentric thoughts, and accept death lovingly.
Surrender to a realized Soul allows us a beautiful death.
For in both we surrender to pure Being.

Surrender removes the ego and silences us,
allowing us to experience our nothingness and our omniscience.
When we understand that we are nothing and know nothing, what is there to say?
Our faith is absolute — we can only bow in profound humility.

It is humility that makes real surrender possible.
The disciple must become a tap firmly attached to the water tank
for the water to flow through them and nourish the world.

The real sign of a disciple is *seva,* service.

Amma usually asks seekers to practice seva
since this is the most suitable practice for the temperament of our age.
Any who are inclined toward asceticism are guided accordingly
and must be ready for sun, rain, cold, hunger and more!
To gain control of the fluctuating mind and experience mental peace
takes intense yearning for the goal, strong aversion to the world and the body,
as well as the ability to tolerate isolation—and all of this is very difficult for most people.
For this reason, Mother recommends selfless service.
When we serve others, our minds expand and we can receive divine grace
and eventually achieve liberation.
In the end, the two paths of asceticism and seva become one.

Service performed for a master is a kind of meditation—its ultimate aim
to learn to love and serve the entire world as our master.
It is more than service since it allows us to forget ourselves
and experience the highest levels of meditation.

For the true disciple, serving the guru is the great joy of one's life.

The light of the guru shines in the disciple's heart like an eternal full Moon,
creating a permanent link with divine Presence.

Impressions made in the earth soon fade and disappear,
but those made in the human heart last forever.
That is why the lives of the great Souls are remembered
long after they have left their bodies.

The guru creates moments so beautiful and memorable
that we cherish them as the sweetest, most precious memories of our lives
and they stay with us forever.

The guru arranges circumstances that create a series of exhilarating and unforgettable
experiences that generate wave upon wave upon wave of pure Love
until finally there is simply nothing but Love.

The vast compassion of the guru allows the disciple to experience
being part of the guru, belonging to the guru, being greatly loved
and knowing that everything that happens is for the highest good.

The guru's compassion is all forgiving.
Enveloping the disciple it soothes away all negative feelings,
allowing the disciple to relax and feel comfortable and receive discipline
in a positive frame of mind.

In the beginning of spiritual life we need discipline.
Discipline is the staircase to the heights of spirituality.

Many people are afraid to take the journey
which involves the death of the ego and the rebirth of the inner child.
Only faith in the guru makes this possible.

Our innocent Love and our faith in the guru help us undertake the awesome journey.

When our inner child awakens, our divine power awakens—
and this is the only power that attracts God.
This power is magnetic and boundlessly generous
and will carry us to the summit—the supreme state of Love.

To really grow, we need a combination of mature conscious surrender to the Master
and innocent childlike reliance on the Mother.
The proportions depend upon the individual and the situation.

As a physician gives different advice to different patients,
a spiritual master must consider the type, condition, character strengths
and weaknesses of the individual disciple.

The master helps us overcome our mental habits,
detach and free ourselves from transitory objects and worldly pleasures,
and find genuine happiness and contentment in the ultimate Truth.

The master's role is to help us realize the insignificance
of this petty thing we call "the ego".

If Mother always showed Love and affection,
we would never look inward and really search for our real Self.

The guru's divine presence and ever-flowing grace
are always purifying the disciple.

Like a gardener tending to a garden of variegated flowers,
Amma does not treat the perfect flowers, only those that are diseased.
She constantly works on her children's weaknesses—
pinching leaves and petals to save a plant or its blossoms.
This may be painful, but it is well worth it!

Our virtuous aspects do not require attention, but if our weaknesses
are not eliminated, they can destroy even our virtues.

Once the master begins to operate, she will not let us go.
What surgeon would let a patient run away before the operation is over?
Since the master is inseparable from God, basking in her overflowing Love
and compassion greatly reduces the pain.

Sometimes we may think that Amma is angry
when She is lovingly removing our weaknesses to further our spiritual progress.

Unaware of the plane on which the enlightened guru functions,
the disciple sometimes becomes impatient, judgmental and critical.
The only thing that helps them then is the master's unconditional Love.

There are many kinds of people — some are like crystal,
others like clay; some are like coal and others are like clay.
When the master tries to refine and remold them, some can be purified,
integrated and elevated in the master's image and become another offering.
Others — like mud parched by the Sun — turn brittle, crumble and disintegrate.
It all depends on the persons level of understanding, attitude and maturity.

The path to God cannot be forced — indeed force can ruin the whole process.
The guru has to be enormously patient in helping the disciple
to open their closed heart into a lovely fragrant flower.

It is the guru's patience that particularly promotes our spiritual growth.

My children, beholding a disciple's virtues, the guru sings a lullaby of compassion.
Oh my darlings, to receive the eternal Guru's grace, do what Mother says!

Once we come to a perfect Master, all our sins are washed away.

So instead of wasting your time thinking, "I am a sinner,"
focus on absorbing the master's teachings.

To attain the spiritual heights takes great inner strength and steadfast concentration.

Steadfastness is an indication of our intense Love for the goal.

To make progress on the path, steadfastness and tireless dedication
are absolutely necessary.

For a true seeker there is no day or night.

A monastic disciple has to become strong enough to shoulder the burdens
of the entire world.

Sincere spiritual seekers pray to eliminate all their negative tendencies
and work hard to accomplish this.

They do not pray for achievements or fulfillment of desires, only to transcend them.
True seekers passionately long to return to their original true home.
Increasingly weighed down by the ego, they experience
a growing and intensifying urge to release it.

Doing practices once a day is insufficient — we need to practice continuously.
Whatever we are doing, wherever we are, we should chant our mantra
or reflect on the eternal truths and teachings.
This is the only way to reach the goal of Self-realization.

For the earnest seeker every action should be viewed as a spiritual practice.

A mind fixed on God will not be ensnared by Maya.

To reach its destination as soon as possible, the express bus makes very few stops.
Continuous remembrance of God is the express bus to Reality.

The weapons of the ego are powerless in the face of karma.
But if we drop to our knees in surrender and lay down our arms
at the Guru's feet, even karma can be escaped!
With divine Grace, the arrow we released in our past life will not harm us.

Aware that a process of purification is underway, true seekers do not run away.
They remain composed in the awareness that they will receive protection
from their practices and can count on the guru's assistance, support and grace.
True seekers try to confront every situation with a discerning mind and intelligence
and never try to break the karmic chain.

As we try to row through the dense river of weeds,
the guru cuts the weeds away and opens the path.
What normally would take several lifetimes is accomplished in one.
With the guru's grace we have only to endure a tenth of our karma—
the guru takes care of the rest.

The true disciple is protected and transformed forever.

Karma is easily overcome by the grace of a perfect Master.
If we follow the Master's instructions, we can triumph over any trial or tribulation.
Faith in the Guru fills our hearts and souls with enormous strength and courage.
With the Guru's guidance and grace, not even Death can touch us.

A perfect Master's mere thought, look or touch
can bring about tremendous transformation.
If such Masters wish, they can bestow Self-realization on a disciple or follower.
They can do anything they wish, since their will is one with God's.

Every mind has it own concepts and based on them, forms judgments
which are not easy to eliminate.
Only the burning heat of *tapas*, created by the master's discipline
and the disciple's loving attachment, has the power to dissolve the mind.
But this process requires enormous patience.

One who has any preferences is not Amma.
To be Amma takes the patience of the tree, the patience of the wind,
the patience of the flowing river—that much patience!

The Love of the guru encompasses patience, forbearance and perseverance.

The nature of the mind is like downward-flowing water.
But Consciousness is like upward-rising fire—
it transports us to the pure Self.

All of Amma's children's actions should be full of pure sweet Love.

It is our Love that transforms our actions into service to the guru.
Only the guru can handle disciples and eliminate their inertia.
Normally we follow mental whims that pull us into the lower depths.
To become conscious of the Self, we need to become like fire
which when pushed down, always rises back up.

Spiritual life is like standing amidst the blazing flames and not burning up.

For the ignorant, still bound by the ego, nothing is harder to know than Reality,
but for those burning to know, nothing is easier.

The I of the ego causes impurities that can only be eliminated by incineration
in the furnace of Love.

The hold of the ego can only be broken by the suffering of pure Love.

Our impurities have to be melted in the heat of our longing for infinite Love
and the agony of our separation and suffering—which we call *tapas*.
In the end, the gopis' longing for Krishna became so intense,
their identification with Him so extreme,
that any separation became literally intolerable—
and their individuality dissolved into Him.

The seeker's Love becomes as consuming as a forest fire — even more so!
The seeker's entire being burns in the raging flames
until finally it is consumed by the One.

Love prepares the mind by driving away all of Love's enemies
so the lover can receive and welcome the Beloved wholeheartedly.
The unhindered heart surges to the Beloved with unquenchable thirst
and unappeasable passion to consume the Beloved
and become Love itself.

At first spiritual Love is beautiful and peaceful, but as our longing to unite intensifies,
it becomes an overwhelming, agonizing, excruciating pain
that will not stop until we merge with the Beloved.
In merging we discover a Love even more glorious than our early Love —
unfading, eternally alive, all around us and within.
There is only Love — Love, lover and beloved are all one now.
In the final stage everything melts into ineffable supreme Love —
and this is where the Master is taking you.

In the early days, Amma never slept.
She stayed awake calling to the Divine,
crying out, praying, meditating and dancing in bliss.
Moonlit nights were her favorite times — on those silent peaceful nights
she was oblivious of everything around her.
Her longing reached such a peak that everything expressed only the Absolute.

So You may dance in me, adorable Mother,
I bow and surrender to You.
If You, the power of Life in every soul, were ever to leave,
there would be only Silence.
Cosmic Energy, Pure Bliss, Supreme Light, come!
Come and never abandon me!
Ocean of Knowledge, Cause of Creation, Foundation of the Universe,
Eternal Essence, Atom of Atoms, All Pervading One!
Dweller in the Thousand-petalled Lotus, come, oh come!
Brilliant as a trillion Suns, You are within me — my only hope, to merge in You.

Ambrosial Light, Ocean of Bliss, may this mind melt and dissolve in You forever!
Absolute Being, to You I bow over and over again.
Compassionate Mother who removes all affliction, remove this agony!
Knowledge of Knowledge, Quintessence, Goddess Shive,
Shelter, Kundalini Shakti Ma!
I do not even know how to know — take all these doubts!
Save me, great Maya, from this madness!

Mother, my Mother, why can't I see you?
I know You hide in this tree, in these plants,
in these animals, these birds.
The whole earth earth is nothing but You.
Oh Mother, concealed in the ocean waves and cooling breeze,
my elusive Mother.

To live in Love means death to the ego,
but once we unite with the Beloved
we experience nothing but Peace, Love, Light and Silence.

Conflict ends and we emanate nothing but pure universal Love.
To attain this state, we have to endure pain—but this is nothing compared
to the endless flow of Bliss that awaits us at the goal.

We cannot approach the Divine without suffering—
spirituality is not for the uncommitted.
Indeed, the suffering on the subtle plane is even greater
than that experienced in the world.

Even in the world the intensity of pain and sacrifice we undergo
depends on the amount of happiness we seek.
Spiritual bliss is the highest, most lasting form of happiness
and therefore the most expensive.
Lower lesser pleasures have to be sacrificed to attain it.

If our goal is Self-realization,
then our ego and personal tastes have to be released.
And this takes real effort—along with the guidance and grace of the guru.

Ascetics who conserve their energy through rigorous practices
are eventually transformed into inexhaustible power sources.
Those who live in constant self indulgence, endless expectations, hopes and dreams,
who drain their energy building castles in the air, eventually break down.
And who will be able to revive them?

The very existence of the world depends upon the spiritual energy
generated by sincere practitioners through their austerities.

While some people act wrongly, others act rightly—
and so society is never entirely destroyed.
Bad is balanced by good, insult by praise, destruction by creation,
enjoyment by abstinence, indulgence by detachment.
On the one hand energy is spent, on the other hand it is saved.

The world cannot exist without give and take.

The simplicity and austerity of monastic life allows others to partake of the world.
The world's very existence depends upon the spiritual energy
generated by the renunciation of true seekers.

Today we live in the Kali Yuga, the Age of Action.
When action is combined with commitment to the spiritual goal,
it becomes the greatest form of renunciation and austerity.

Only through surrender can we ever realize the Self.
For true disciples everything in the universe becomes a guru.
Without this attitude, we cannot learn anything,
no matter how many experiences we have.

Longing for God and humility before others are the signs of true discipleship.

India's ancient masters, viewed as God,
were simple and humble — as were their disciples.

It was their mutual Love and humility that made the direct
heart-to-heart transmission of Knowledge possible.
United they prayed for guidance and protection by the Truth.
And Knowledge rose from the depths of their Love and was revealed.

A truly great Soul is the incarnation of pure Humility.

A true guru lives the eternal Truths and a true disciple, observing the guru,
sincerely tries to live them too.

A true disciple is an instrument that spreads the master's Knowledge.

A true disciple is a conduit that carries the master's Wisdom to the world.

A disciple who is truly aware, devoted and surrendered
receives the guru's message and guidance wherever he or she goes.

Eventually the whole universe becomes the guru.

True seekers put their energy into going deeper and deeper into their Consciousness.
They do not worry about the fruits of their actions.
They surrender entirely to God, concentrate on their practices
and let everything unfold naturally—they do not resist.

True seekers understand that their life is an arrow that has already left the bow.
The song must be sung to the end, and it is their own voice that must sing it.
We have to face this, no matter how painful it may be.

The seedling rises only after the shell has broken.
The Self rises only after the ego has cracked.
Like a seedling under growing pressure from a cramping shell,
our growing desire for Light and liberation will finally burst the ego.
Whatever pain this causes is nothing compared to the glory of the mature tree—
the shell will be irrelevant.

Once we are really aware of the Self, the ego loses all meaning.

Only when the disciple goes beyond the self-imposed limitations of individuality
and merges with the Self—which is none other than the guru—
can the guru be truly known.

Dedicate everything to Mother as your all-in-all—take everything as her will.
Or have faith in your Self and inquire within, knowing you are the all-pervading Self.
Intent on the goal, become conscious of all your actions.

My children, the Goddess you worship when you chant *Om Amriteswaryai namah*,
is the essential nectar of the immortal Self
in the thousand-petaled Lotus at the crown of your head.
That is what we are striving for—not a five-foot body!
Discover your own inner Power.
Discover the Bliss that is within you.
This is the meaning of *Om Amriteswaryai namah*.

When we reach that Perfection, we will understand that the real Self
always has been and always will be—
beyond birth and death and the law of karma.

Oh divine Spirit, do You see me here?
May your starry hands shower grace upon me.
Grant me the strength to keep remembering You
and the sorrow to keep calling You,
my only refuge and comfort.
Blissful, oh beautiful is your divine World!
Lift me to your World of a billion trillion twinkling stars.

Our real birthday is the day that we realize:
We were never born and we will never die.

18
REALIZATION

My children, Self-realization
is the ability to see yourself in all beings.

To know your Self is to see others as part of your Self
and experience others' joy and sorrow as your own.

Ultimately no one is different from anyone else—
a thousand pots of water will reflect the same Sun.

All created beings are one with life and have the same life purpose.
To achieve that universal purpose, we must direct our energy
toward realizing our universal nature.

We can only be fulfilled by directing our energy toward realizing our own true nature.

The real purpose of life is to experience what is beyond our physical existence.
Most people think of life as a struggle for survival and ask only
for a decent job, income, home, spouse and children.
But there is a higher purpose: To know and realize who we really are!

Whatever our responsibilities in the world, they should always help us
fulfill our higher responsibility to experience our unity
with the Supreme Being of the universe.

Since the universal Soul is infinite,
all our individual views are bound to be incorrect!
Only when they are gone
can the supreme Soul reveal Itself to us.

At this stage, our minds are so gross that we cannot even imagine
a changeless, formless God devoid of attributes.
Thus we need some form like Buddha, Krishna or Christ
to show us our own divine qualities.

To reveal the supreme Reality to human beings, God assumes a human form
because this is the only way we can begin to grasp the Truth.

Knowledge of God and the goal of Self-realization are not really different.

Pure Being appears in human form to guide the ignorant onto the path of Goodness.

The voice of the guru awakens the disciple from a deep hibernation—
and what does it say? "A new age is being born
and you are to be its creator. Awaken!
Arise and joyfully take on the sacrifice and surrender.
This will not be a burden—it will give you the wings to soar
in the realm of your own true Self."

To protect dharma, boundless formless Being assumes a variety of finite forms
that in time dissolve back into the Infinite.

We cannot know when, where or how the glory of God will manifest.
Unlimited, undivided by time or space, It can incarnate at any time and in any place.

Every form is limited—an Incarnation in infinite Reality is like an iceberg in the ocean.

A water tap is not a reservoir, but a reservoir passes through it.
Pure Being is inseparable from an Incarnation.
Through a small body It can do whatever It pleases.
Being needs no body to act, but an Incarnation helps humanity
to approach pure Being.

When people receive an embrace from Amma, it is not a simple physical embrace.
The Love Amma feels for Creation flows out and purifies them,
helping them to awaken and grow spiritually, and arousing in them
the maternal qualities so critically needed today.

Amma is accustomed to large crowds and anyone who is able to wait will receive her darshan.
She can give darshan to forty thousand people while seated for twenty-four hours.
A large crowd in America is a vacation compared to crowds elsewhere.
All this is possible because Amma knows She is one with the central Source of energy
and does not need to be recharged like a battery.

Gurus and great Souls are masters of the mind and utterly free of desire.
Victorious over the mind through perpetual self-sacrifice,
they are blissful, ever poised and perfectly free.

Through extreme sacrifice and austerity the great Souls have eliminated the ego.
No longer identified with the body, the mind or the intellect,
they are permanently established in Supreme Being.

Full realization requires devotion, detachment and knowledge.
Eventually the Yamuna of Devotion, the Ganges of Detachment and the Saraswati
of Knowledge converge in the holy River Triveni — and the three become one.

A Knower of the Self has dissolved the mind completely
through incessant and intense spiritual practices.
As a result the mind is fully fixed on the Supreme.
Because a Knower is one with That, everything is seen as That.
When the Knower views an object, it is not the external appearance
that is seen but What illumines it.
For the Knower everything is pure Being.
When speaking, the Knower speaks only to That.

A staircase is only necessary until we reach the top.
Once we reach our goal we go beyond the means—
the faith or religion that lead us there.
Once we go beyond, we can either return to lift up other souls
or we can dissolve into the Infinite.

Children, once full realization is attained
most souls merge into Eternity—only a very few return.
Who upon entering the Ocean of Bliss would ever want to leave?

Most souls prefer to remain in the impersonal state—
ignoring the calls and cries of seekers and sufferers.
To return from that state of no return takes monumental determination and willpower.
Only a few rare souls—because of their phenomenal Love, compassion,
and desire to serve humanity—can accomplish the colossal task.

The Love of a great Soul is utterly beyond words.
What we see and experience externally—as intense and profound as that may be—
is only an infinitesimal fraction of Its intensity and depth.
We could speak and write about it endlessly
and never come up with an adequate description—
because that Love is vaster than the universe and knows no limit.

The presence of a realized master is an extremely profound blessing to the world.
But only the rarest of these—out of their boundless Love, power and knowledge—
can embrace the entire world with outstretched arms of compassion.
These are the Avatars, the Divine Incarnations
who are born with full awareness of their divine nature.

An Avatar is an incarnation of the universal Mind.

Avatar means "to descend".
Infinite Consciousness "descends" to the world to assume a human form —
or so it seems from the perspective of a follower.
In reality, there is no place for Consciousness to ascend or descend to.
How can omnipresent, all-pervasive Being ascend or descend
when It is already here?
Concepts such as "descent" arise before we have experienced
Oneness with the supreme Reality.
Once we merge into that ocean of pure Life Energy
known as Being-Awareness-Bliss,
concepts of coming and going have no meaning.

Once a Soul "descends" from union with God, the
role of living and working to elevate humanity is played to the very end.
Problems, obstacles, challenges, scandals, slander and abuse are plentiful,
but a great Soul remains indifferent to it all.

Seemingly like other people, such Souls are really totally different.
Merged in the Truth, they are untouched by life.

To express Love and compassion, be of service and inspire others to develop
their divine qualities, a body is needed.
Once a Soul takes a body, it runs its natural course.
A God-realized Soul gives their body to the world.
But it is no ordinary body—it can be used to do extraordinary things
without suffering and illness, as long as desired.
Great Souls make their bodies undergo ordinary human experiences—
and therein lies their true greatness.

Jesus and Krishna could easily have prevented the events that destroyed their bodies.
Instead they surrendered and let their bodies react naturally.
Being omnipotent, they could have avoided all those bitter experiences
and effortlessly destroyed their opponents, but they chose to set an example
and show humanity that it is possible to uphold the highest values
under any circumstances.

If an Avatar practices severe austerities
it is not because He or She needs to, but because an example is needed
to inspire and elevate humanity.

Living among humans and undergoing the hardships of life,
an Avatar will always set an example of Love, compassion and sacrifice.
In so doing, He or She becomes a powerful source of inspiration
for millions of people all over the world.

Though externally Jesus was a man, internally He was a mother.
In Him, abstract formless Love became concrete.
Jesus gave his life to Love and taught humanity how to love—
though his message has mostly been misinterpreted by those who have tried to convey it.
To really understand the nature of Christ, one would have to undergo
the same austerities that He underwent.
Only those who follow his path perfectly know what He truly is.

The greatest sacrifice that Christ made
was to live among ordinary animalistic people
in order to transform them into God.

Through the lives of the great Souls, ordinary people experience
holiness, grace, enlightenment and bliss.
Because of their lives, culture and morality flourish.

The Incarnations are the epoch-makers whose lives bring about
a moral, cultural and spiritual renaissance on Earth.

Some of a seeker's diseases are incinerated by the fires of Knowledge,
but others must be experienced.
The bodies of both sinners and saints must suffer.
The suffering of the great Souls is intended to teach renunciation.

An Incarnation's life of renunciation, Love, compassion and selflessness
inspires humanity to want to experience the same way of life.

By their mere glance, touch, word or even thought, an Incarnation can transmit
immense spiritual power, burn off negative personality traits
and bestow ultimate freedom.

The great Souls are an endless source of Love and compassion.
Like gigantic batteries of inexhaustible energy
they are constantly charged with power from the Source.
Only those who have totally merged in God have the power to save the world.

A realized Soul exists at the highest level — the supreme peak — of Consciousness.
In the presence of such a Soul, psychic wounds spontaneously heal
and sorrow suddenly vanishes.

True Masters and Incarnations dwell in the bliss of pure Being —
unlimited and faultless as boundless space.
Bearing the burdens of the world to ease its suffering,
Masters and Incarnations dispel the darkness of delusion and ignorance
and kindle the light of Self-knowledge in the human heart.

The manifestation of a divine Incarnation is like the full Moon rising on a dark night.
Its beauty and impact cannot be overstated—
every level of life is touched and nourished.
The ordinary, yet extraordinary life of Sri Krishna is a perfect example.
Human yet divine, Krishna demonstrated what it is to be a complete human being.

When we transcend the mind completely, we become complete.
Lord Krishna accomplished this and is thus said to be a *Purnavatara* or full Incarnation.
Smilingly He moved from circumstance to circumstance
as if simply moving from one room to another—like the wind blowing freely,
touching and caressing everyone everywhere—uncontainable.

Krishna's life was a song with a charming rhythm
and a beautiful melody sung in perfect pitch.
We can see the fullness of his life in his teachings as well.
Relevant today for people of all walks of life, they show us how to advance
both materially and spiritually.

In a perfect Master, we can see and know the eternal virtues of Love,
respect, equanimity, renunciation, patience, forbearance, endurance and selflessness.
A perfect Master's only desire is the welfare of Creation.

Since true Masters are beyond personal taste and preference,
they can offer Love and compassion to everyone—
even those who attack and insult them.

Realized Masters who dwell in pure Being are not disturbed by life's experiences.
Masters of the mind and senses, they can manifest any godly quality
and withdraw unaffected and detached.

That supreme state of Consciousness is like the Sun
shining on a mirror—to know Itself.

One with the source of Energy, an Incarnation works tirelessly to soothe and heal
the deep wounds of all who come—to give peace and joy to all.

Great Souls who embody Love and compassion are as patient as the Earth,
but when they are angry, their anger goes extremely deep.

For the fully realized Master, perfectly complete in Themselves,
nothing remains to be gained or lost.
How can such a master need adoration, praise, fame or followers?

The wealthiest people in the world are the spiritual Masters
who contain the whole Universe within them.

Only spiritual Souls who have conserved a huge amount of energy
can afford to give lavishly from their limitless supply.
Only those who save their energy for the world, can help those in need.
Only those who renounced attachment, can be blissful in every circumstance.
Patient and forbearing, persevering and forgiving—they are beyond.
Forever joyful in the Self, they are unaffected by time or place—
in a wild forest or the depths of hell, they are happy.

A fully realized spiritual Master is a master of Creation itself.

A real guru is always in a state of oneness with the Supreme
and has no sense whatsoever of *I* or *mine*.
Once the ego is gone, the body is merely an empty shell unconnected to the Self.

A real guru is not the body—though that is not precisely true either
since the body is all that we can see.
In reality a great spiritual Master is a presence like the endless sky.

The world cannot understand the great Masters.
People want to destroy what they cannot understand with the ordinary intellect.
For it seems strange, unreasonable and illogical—the ego cannot tolerate it!
We fear that the ego will be demolished,
and we want the ego and the world to go on forever,
so we can keep on possessing, acquiring, enjoying and indulging—
which we consider to be the whole point of living.

Great Souls, undivided and whole, are strangers to this world.
Ordinary people will not permit them to live freely, speaking the Truth.
They try to bind and chain them, but it does not work.

Over and over, the life of Christ demonstrated that society rewards
a follower of Truth with a crown of thorns.
All great Souls necessarily face many difficulties,
but knowing the Truth from their own experience
they do not give up and cannot be stopped.

Sri Krishna, Sri Rama and Jesus Christ all had to undergo many challenges
which they boldly faced without breaking down.
They converted every obstacle into a stepping-stone — and therein lies their greatness.
They showed with their very lives that when we make a sincere effort
to reach a higher goal, no force in the world can stop us.
After thousands of years, their lives still inspire us to be strong.

Real Mahatmas are never bound by institutions.
They go forth holding the supreme Truth as their only ideal.

Try to understand that great Souls do not come here to destroy anything—
they come to create a positive, healthy, intelligent way of life.

Today, the all-pervading infinite Consciousness and inexhaustible Energy
that once incarnated as Rama and Krishna has reincarnated in a new form.

Amma's life shows that it is possible to realize the Supreme Being
under the worst possible circumstances.

Amma is not here to rest in comfort, but to serve and reduce human suffering.
Your happiness is her happiness.
Amma does not need to be served—She is here to serve.

Amma's wealth is to see her children happy.

Children, Mother needs nothing from you but the burden of your sorrow.
She is here to carry it.

What Amma does is not work — it is worship.

Amma sees hidden within each of you an Amma, a Krishna, a Buddha or a Christ.
Divine Light can dawn at any moment — it simply waits for the right time.
Great masters can see the Light waiting to burst through the walls of the ego.
They behold a future divine Incarnation in everyone.

For Amma, there is no such thing as a God seated on some throne up in Heaven.
God is the all-pervading Consciousness that animates all things.
God is each and every one of you.
People, plants, animals, trees, mountains and rivers — are all Amma's God.

Seeing the divine Mother in you,
Amma bows down to her own Self — the Supreme.

For Amma, all are her masters.
Everything in this world — grass, worms, everything —
is master and God for Amma.

Amma sees only the pure essence within you,
and with practice you can become like Her.

Amma is the servant of servants.

Amma is the servant of each of you.
She has no special dwelling—She dwells in your hearts.

As long as Amma can continue to reach out to those who come to her,
as long as She has the strength to embrace, console and wipe away tears,
She will continue to do so.

To lovingly caress, console and wipe away others' tears until the very end
of this mortal frame—that is Amma's wish.

Amma is not doing anything.
She feels she is using her right arm to caress her left.
Amma's mission is to help humanity understand this Truth.

This body is here only because Amma is in it.

The external Amma that you see now
is like the reflection of a flower in a bowl of water.

Though people may call her visible form Amma,
the indwelling Self has no name or address—it extends everywhere.

Amma is pure Consciousness.

When Amma meditates, She sees her own Self.

The Light that we depict as a halo is knowledge of the true Self.

No matter what happens, Amma is always at peace.

Amma is here to achieve certain goals that will benefit humanity
and is confident that they will be achieved.

Amma has no fear.

This is Amma's path.

Now we behold only the outer lamp,
but within Mother burns a Light that will never be extinguished.

The Self that is in me is also in you.
Once you realize that the Indivisible is always shining in you,
you will become That too.

Once you realize the truth of Existence,
your individual self will no longer exist.

Those who realize the true Self see It in everyone and feel only compassion.

When Amma sees and embraces people,
She does not only see their outer appearance—She sees God.
As the honeybee sees honey in the flowers,
Amma sees the nectar of Love in human beings.

For Amma, everyone is beautiful.

Amma is never bored—in real Love how can there ever be boredom?
Everything is fresh—Amma lives totally in the present.
For the mother whose heart is full of Love, everything her child does is beautiful.

Because people call me Mother,
I call them children.

Amma never asked anyone to call Her Mother.
People do this spontaneously and Amma responds by calling them children.
Mother does not care what people call Her.
Devotees and seekers say Amma, others use her given name,
atheists and other opponents call Her unflattering, insulting names—
but it does not matter, it is not important.
What people see is determined by their own personality.
The body changes and dies—whatever you call it, This does not care.
This came from the Unconditional—bodiless, It manifested in a body
called by many names, but always unaffected and unchanged.
No one can pierce the mystery of this Being.

The higher we rise, the more the mind will expand.
When we attain the heights, we will see everything as One
and will not be disturbed by any differences.

As our Love becomes subtler, it becomes more powerful.
As it deepens, we rise farther up until we are finally totally identified
with our Beloved and realize that we are not separate but One.
That is the final step—the summit of Love.

Mother is beyond aspects, unconfined by states and moods,
and does not make such distinctions.
Even the role of Goddess, Amma adopted at the urging of her devotees
who surrendered to it and reveled in it.

Mother is like a pristine lake—whoever wishes to bathe, may do so;
whoever wishes to drink and quench their thirst, may do so;
whoever wishes to spit, may do so.

For Amma, everything is the Self.
She is here for the sake of the world.
Her only aim is to lead people to the Truth.
To lift up humanity is her only desire.

The river of the master has no ego and does not think:
"I am flowing, I am powerful and beautiful, I can take you to the ocean—
look at all the people bathing, swimming and delighting in me!"
The river simply flows because that is its nature.

A great Soul is like a lake of crystal-clear pure water
from whose rock-solid foundation a spring eternally gushes forth
producing ever more fresh water.
The spring never dries up—the lake is forever full for anyone to take a drink.
The great Soul realizes She is the changeless indestructible Atman,
the immovable bedrock of the cosmos,
the never-ending source of Love and compassion.

Love is Mother's nature and the only way She can be.
Mother can do nothing but bestow boundless compassion and Love upon others.
Egolessness is Nothingness filled with Love and Divinity.
Anger, hatred, abuse dissolve in the ocean of Mother's compassion.

When all are finally disarmed, She will be victorious.

Mother is not attached to her achievements.
At any moment She can go—shedding her skin like a snake.
While here She keeps trying to help people—that is all.

The goal of a divine Incarnation is to lead humanity to its highest Self—
that Essence inherent in every individual.

The life goal of every great Soul is to help humanity discover heaven within
and show that good actions will bring us closer to God.

To teach and discipline the world and guide it back to the Path,
great Masters create an apparent ego, which they totally surpass.
But within, they remain untouched, pure, innocent and eternally silent.
The life and teachings of great Souls are practical reminders of the real purpose of life.

Great Souls do not live for themselves but for the good of the world.
Their example awakens the goodness within us
and helps us to be compassionate, overcome our selfishness,
repent when we are angry, pray to be forgiving, and want to be loving.

The Supreme is far beyond any describable attributes or characteristics,
but to help the mind grasp It, we say It has the qualities reflected in the great Souls—
truthfulness, responsibility, self-sacrifice, compassion and Love.
These qualities actually are God, and as we develop them we come to know God.
When we renounce the ego, they reflect from us like a mirror—
the human heart reflects the beauty of God.

Great Souls live forever through their selfless actions.
Even if you cannot accomplish as much, always do what you can for others.

A great Soul is a soft breeze comforting to all.

Amma cannot hate anyone.
A great Soul cannot hate, only love —
doing otherwise is impossible.

Amma would vote in elections if She could vote for every candidate.
She is a mother — how can a mother pick one of her children over another?

For Amma, there is nothing to reject — Love accepts everything.
Anyone who aspires to the spiritual heights must learn to love and respect everyone
and consider everyone's feelings and problems their own.

Amma's aim is to give her children the Love and strength they need.
Once we release our personal likes and dislikes and liberate ourselves from our minds,
we too will become living vessels of grace and a blessing to the world.

Try to remember that Amma is within everybody —
that is how She knows everything.

Mother dwells in you and in the subtlest particles of the Earth.

When you know who you are, you will know who I am.

What Amma does is for the benefit of the whole world.

Amma has come to bring Love to the world.

Do not look at what Amma does externally—that is not the real Amma.
The real Amma is inside each of you.
Do not be fooled by the outer leela, the divine play.

We can only experience a part of the infinite Love and compassion
showered upon us by a great Soul—to experience more
we have to look beyond the dazzling outer manifestation.

Amma is a representation of God.

As a mother knows the meaning of her toddler's glances, garbled words
and silent moods, the Great Mother knows the desires
of all her devotees without being told.
Perhaps She prefers the prayers of quiet empty minds
to the prayers of those swarming with desires,
and that is why they call Her Mookambika, the silent Mother of pure Energy
who knows and does everything in Silence, unattached and untouched
as the endless sky—perpetual Witness to everything.

Love is the feeling that I and my life belong to my Beloved—
the feeling of total surrender.

We cannot feel this for what is changing, only for what is unchanging and unending.
True Love is the irrepressible longing for Being itself.
Only through perfect surrender can that pure and selfless Bliss be known.
To know such happiness we must dedicate our life to That.

Divine Mother caressed my head with her gentle radiant hands.
And I bowed, offering my life to Her.
Smiling and dazzling brilliantly, She dissolved into Me.
Bathed in the rainbow-light of Divinity, my Mind burst into bloom.
All the events of millions of years rose up within Me.
Nothing was apart from my Self—all was One.
Merged in Her I relinquished all pleasure.
"Teach humanity to realize its purpose," She told Me.
And I proclaim to the world the sublime Truth She uttered:
Humanity, merge in your Self!

Amma prays that all her children will be blessed with the mental strength
and physical health to attain the Goal in this lifetime.

Amma has always been with you
and will never leave you.

19
SUPREME SELF

It is true that the divine Self is within us.

We have everything within us.

You will never find more pure Being somewhere in India—
or even in heaven—than in you.

You do not need to go searching for divine Consciousness
because It shines in everyone!

We are kings and queens who unwittingly live like beggars
when the entire universe already belongs to us.

Throw away your begging bowl and discover the bounty within you!

Never hesitate to call upon that divine Strength,
which is not outside but within you.
Awaken your innate power!

We are all supreme Consciousness.
Being ignorant of the soul and worshipping the body is like
being ignorant of the electricity and imagining appliances run on their own.

It is foolish to rely on human power alone, no matter how impressive it seems to be.
Never forget the divine Power within you that is your true strength.

Spiritual life has only one purpose:
to relinquish what is not really us
and become what we really are.

We are a boundless scintillating ocean of Knowledge and Beauty
whose waves encircle each other in a glorious round
and break on the shores of life.

Our real nature is like the sky, not the clouds—like the ocean, not the waves.
Clouds and waves are passing—sky and ocean are lasting.

We identify with our passing emotions
but we are not those puffy clouds—
we are the wide open sky!

We are not candles that need to be lit—we are the self-effulgent Sun.
We are the embodiments of supreme Consciousness.

All we need to do is realize this!
We are Love.

If we really believe we embody Love
and strive to know and manifest this,
the gates to supreme Power will open within us.

The body is a divine gift full of amazing mysteries—
the transformation of food into blood, the capacity to heal itself
and the power to know the supreme Reality.

The body and the mind are the instruments of spiritual practice
and have to be kept healthy to function well.
Otherwise they will become the cause of much suffering.

Today the human race is moving in a direction opposite to the goal of Self-awakening.

Although we call ourselves human beings, we still have the minds of animals.
They need to evolve and become truly human before we can realize the Supreme Self
and ascend to godliness—in accordance with the course of divine evolution.

Realization is not some special realm we reach after death.
The animal mind needs to shift to a human mind for us to rise and attain divinity.
This inner resurrection is what is meant by the realization of the Self.

What makes us different from the animals
is the transcendence of our childish innocence—
by means of our discriminating intelligence and detachment—
to a conscious knowledge of our absolute Innocence.

If we do not go beyond childlike innocence to become human, we will remain animals.

Spirituality is a journey from innocence to Innocence.

A child is innocent but also ignorant.
The innocence of Self-realization, Knowledge and Awareness is true Innocence.

The innocence of a child is like a deep sleep—
the innocence of Self-awareness is an awakening.
Our first innocence is a temporary boon from Mother Nature—
our final innocence a permanent and indestructible realization of our eternal Nature.

Life is a great journey back to pure Consciousness.

We are the source of unlimited supreme Power
and to understand this is the goal of life.

The purpose of every life is to experience this limitless power as one's true Self.

No one should miss the divine flight to the Self!

May we uncover our own inner Power —
the blissful Joy forever within us.

May we depend on our divine Power and realize our immense Strength.
We are not meek little lambs but majestic powerful Lions!

We think that we are finite batteries, but when we discover our connection
to the Infinite we discover that we are limitless.

Once we know that we are That Self,
we are like batteries connected to the power source of the Universe.

Self-confidence is the booster rocket that enables us to soar
to the heights of spirituality.

An atom bomb can reduce a whole continent to ashes even though its power
comes from atoms so small they can only be seen under a microscope.

A tall leafy banyan tree emerges from a tiny seed.
The essence of God inhabits everything in existence.
With reason, experience and commitment to a path of awakening this Power
we will discover our own true Essence.

When our inner vision is corrected through spiritual practice,
the light of pure Knowledge will dawn.

For those who become enlightened, the entire universe is seen as One.

When we dive deep into the true Self
we discover the thread of Love that binds everything together.
Once that is found, all discord melts into pure peace.

The suffering in this world is caused only by the ego.
In God's world there is no suffering.

Once the ego is gone, we will simply flow like a river.

Once our ignorance is gone, sorrow goes too.
Boil your tears down to one drop
and offer it to God.
Become pure, my children.

Just as the electricity keeps flowing when a refrigerator breaks down,
the Soul flows on forever.

When we have no ego, we are everything.

To surrender, to offer yourself and sacrifice your ego
takes great courage—indeed, real daring.

The small I must die into the big I.

Knowing your Self is like peeling an onion until nothing remains.

Surrender cannot be learned from books, people or schools.
As Love keeps growing, the ability to surrender keeps growing too.
In the end, all must surrender to the great Self in whom we have our being—
the Self that we truly are.

When we go beyond the ego and find our true Self,
we shed our desires and experience peace and harmony in the world.

Spiritual people are like the wind—
experiencing the One, our minds expand, our hearts unfold
and Love spreads throughout Creation.

When we surrender everything to the Supreme,
the past loses its grip and slips away—leaving us in a beautiful present,
immersed in the enchanting form of God.

All our nightmares vanish and we are constantly guided by divine grace.

When we realize that we are not this body but pure Consciousness,
the center of our existence shifts to our real Self.
We wake and realize that all along we have only been dreaming and playing—
and we burst into laughter at the exquisite play of supreme Consciousness.

Once we see everything in life as play, we are as happy going down as going up.
Experiencing life as a swing, we do not fall apart on the downswing.

Life is a blessing, not a punishment.
It is an opportunity to grow, become stronger,
develop positive thoughts, and serve others.

A human life is the greatest blessing, yet we experience so much unhappiness.
This shocks and pains Amma—it is really only self-pity.

The obstacles we encounter in life nourish our spiritual strength and growth
and help our hearts to flower in beauty.

Everyone must walk the path and overcome the obstacles.
To realize our oneness with the Supreme may take a lifetime — or even several.
We have to put in constant effort — it is the only way.
No effort is ever wasted — it all comes back to us as divine grace.

With the right knowledge and the right effort, we can receive grace.

The path that leads to Self-realization is narrow and we walk it alone.
Our progress is usually slow and incremental.
But if we keep on trying with patience, enthusiasm and faith,
we will eventually reach the goal.

Each of us has the key to the vast treasure inside us,
but it is rusted from lack of use.

Like a rusty key, our deeply engrained personal habits must be cleaned off
and rubbed with grease to expose our underlying true being.

It takes time, effort and divine grace to reach the goal.

The more dedicated we are in our effort, the more our hearts will open to Love.
The more Love we give, the more grace we will receive—
and that is what will finally carry us to the goal.

As our Love becomes more subtle, it becomes more powerful.
As our Love deepens, we rise higher and higher
until finally we are utterly identified with the Beloved
and realize that we are not separate but One.
This is the final step to the apex of Love.

Love is like a ladder.
Most people stay on the lowest rung—but do not linger there!

Keep climbing, one step at a time,
from the lowest emotion to the purest form of Love
and the highest state of Being.

Never think "I cannot do it," no matter how difficult it is.

Even if there are potholes in the road, keep trying to move forward.

If we have the right attitude, the guru will remove the obstacles on the road
and steer us into the express-lane to Enlightenment.

A river is bound by two banks, but only one riverbed lies between them.
We may speak of God and believer, master and disciple,
but only Love can unite us with the Self.
Pray "May I love You" and forget everything else.

Such devotion will lead to real success in life.

Love is the wealth that lasts—the well of divine Bliss.

Divine Will is behind every victory and every failure.
Once we realize this, our efforts will succeed.
The purpose of life is to see God in every thought and action—in everything!

Everything that exists is made by God
except for the ego, which is made by man.

The ego is the only thing that human beings create
and the only thing we need to renounce.
Once it is gone there is only divine Creation—
we become a flute on God's lips.

When *I* disappears, only your Self remains.
Then, just as the right hand spontaneously flies to soothe the left when it is hurt,
we spontaneously move to love and serve others when they are hurt.
This is the right and dharmic way of life.

Once we drop the *I*, only *Thou* remains.

Absolute Oneness is the fundamental principle of life.
Long ago the sages said, "God is nowhere but here."
This is the great Truth that pervades everything.
A fire burns in each of us to know that I and the universe are one.

The Supreme Self is everywhere—it is not some distant entity.
Nearer than the nearest, It is unimaginably close.
Shake off your identification with the body, transcend and awaken.
Find out what nearer than the nearest means.

We ourselves are the absolute Self, but it is not enough to say this.
To know it, we have to experience it.

Most of our experiences are fleeting as a dream and occur only on the mental level.
Do not focus on them, try to go beyond.

The Supreme Self is beyond all attributes — It is infinite.

The Supreme Self is pure Experience and pure Bliss.

The universal Self cannot be understood, only experienced.

Have faith in your Self — everything is already in you.

You are the Seer who gazes through your eyes.

Children, we are the divine Light —
the eternally free, infinite and blissful true Self.
Proceed with innocence, effort and faith,
and you will discover the bliss of the Self within you.

There is a divine spark in everyone.

Happiness is inherent in all of us.
Childlike innocence fades with time,
but try to preserve, cultivate and strengthen it.

We should feel happy as little children playing in a pool
while our Mother watches over us.

We are the Self and should never be unhappy,
for our true nature is Bliss.

Everything we do should be blissful.

It is not what we do, but our mental attitude that determines
whether we feel happy or unhappy.

When we are unhappy, we close ourselves to the flow of life.
When we are open and happy, we attract Love.

We do not need anything from the outside—everything is already inside us.

God Consciousness permeates everything.

God is your true Self and your truest Friend.

Divine Consciousness is the Eye of your eye.
the Ear of your ear
and the Mind of your mind.

Awaken to the knowledge that *I am the Supreme Self,
I am unlimited, I have infinite potential.*

If we really want to do something, we can.
The feeling that we are too weak, that the task is too hard
and meant for somebody special, that God is "none of my business"—
is not that of a true seeker.

We are all endowed with the beauty and power of a saint or a sage.
We are infinite sources of Power.
That is why Vedanta advises us to contemplate: *I am the Supreme Self,
I am God, I am the Universe—I am the absolute Power and pure Consciousness
that gives life, beauty and luminosity to all things.*

The word impossible is a curse on humanity—we should get rid of it!
Work hard and discover that nothing is impossible.

We are divinity not yet manifested.
Potent within us is holy, fragrant, eternal Beauty
but a false pride keeps our hearts closed.

We have not yet realized that we exist in Consciousness Itself.
Through our spiritual practices the bud of the heart will slowly loosen its petals.
One day, we will come to know our true identity as supreme Consciousness.

Consider yourself an instrument of God's work and you will receive what you need.
Perform your actions as worship and accept everything as divine grace.
Never lay down the flashlight of Self-awareness.
Remember, nothing exists but the Self.

In truth, we are all embodiments of *Satchidananda:*
Existence, Consciousness and Bliss.
We fail to experience this because of our petty concept of I.

Invoke the glory and splendor of God and It will enter your heart and reveal Itself.
You will realize It was always present—just waiting for your call.

We are not candles waiting to be lit—we are the self-effulgent Sun—
we are incarnations of the supreme Consciousness.
All we need to do, is awaken to this Truth.

Let us awaken from our sleep and always stay awake—
even when our bodies are sleeping.

Children, everything is already within us.
We are masters of the elements—by a mere look or touch
they will become whatever we wish.
Do not think, "It happened to You, Mother, but it can never happen to me,
with all my defects and weaknesses—only if You grant it, can it happen."
Liberation is not something granted—it arises from within!

Awakening has to come from within, and trying to force it
would be like trying to hatch an egg externally—which would simply kill it.
Slow gestation is necessary for the creation of new life.

We desire the Truth, but sometimes the intellect swallows it and we temporarily forget.
We have to keep reawakening our desire for the Truth.

Make a little room — a little is enough — and God will flow in.

The realization of the soul of every single creature is only a matter of time.

For some, Realization has already occurred;
for others, it can occur at any time;
for still others, it will come later.
Because it has not happened yet and may not happen in this lifetime,
do not mistakenly think that it will never happen.

The moment of revelation experienced by many great Souls can happen to you too.
Everyone is being prepared to drop their worldly attachments and ego
and reach the final state.
This has to happen — it is the final stage of evolution — it is inevitable.

We can try to avoid it consciously or unconsciously,
but sooner or later we will lose our grip on things, wealth, body—
everything we think is ours.

Even though we keep thinking we will live forever in the body,
we are constantly becoming more conscious, and eventually all the obstacles
to peace and contentment start falling away.
One day the ego drops and we stop struggling.
We do not protest or pause to think about what to do—
we simply bow in utter surrender.

Deep within, every soul is waiting for the great letting-go.
Most of us do not feel it because our level of consciousness is so low,
but one day that urgency will assert itself.

The divine Self sees everything we do.
Maybe we cannot see Her but She is always here,
guiding us—holding the reins of our life.

At first She uses a long lead and we do not realize that She is in charge.
As we proceed through life, the reins grow shorter and shorter.
One day we discover we cannot move another inch and are totally helpless.
We feel Her tugging at the reins, drawing us inescapably toward Her.
Even if we struggle, we know the Power that pulls us is not of this world
and we have no choice but to surrender.
We are going home to the source of our Existence.
The journey is inevitable and we can only keep moving forward.

The Great Goddess is both knowledge and ignorance.
Knowledge leads to Truth; ignorance leads to untruth and suffering.
Because She is everything, She is knowledge, She is ignorance
and She is the final Truth underlying both.

Maya is simply the mind, not an outer force.
It is the mind's basic structure, and it causes both bondage and liberation.

Time and space are circular not linear.

As the Earth circles the Sun in a regular cycle, Nature circles in cycles too.
The seasons pass in a round—spring, summer, fall, winter—and round they go again.
From the seed comes the tree; from the tree comes the seed.
Human beings cycle from birth to childhood to youth to old age to death and rebirth.
We experience the results of our actions as our karma—until the mind
finally grows quiet and the Soul rests peacefully and contentedly in the Self.

We tangibly experience supreme Consciousness in the singing cuckoo,
the cawing crow, the rumbling ocean, the roaring lion.
It walks in our feet, works in our hands, speaks with our tongues,
sees through our eyes and beats in our hearts.
Consciousness fills everything everywhere and acts through us.
Let us, then, become that supreme Consciousness.

Self-realization is not a realm that we reach after death—it is an inner resurrection.

The supreme Reality is pure Consciousness, pure Awareness.
And once we transcend the differences, we see that It pervades everything.

Amma once said that God is all-pervading and within us—
now She sees everything as God.
God is inside and outside the veil of the physical I—
and the veil is also God.
Once we reach the plane of pure Consciousness
only the Indescribable exists.

On the one hand, God does not have attributes or form.
On the other, It has them since every form is pervaded by God.

There is no way to describe the nature or the characteristics of pure Being.
It can only be known through direct experience.

Yoga, the yoking of the individual to the Supreme Self,
cannot be described in words.
It is ineffable Bliss.

Can words convey the taste of honey or the beauty of Nature?
We only know them by seeing and tasting them.
Pure Being is beyond words, beyond limits—
in everything everywhere whether sentient or insentient.

All the gods and goddesses are different entities,
different faces of one infinite Reality.
The same Power inhabits them all.

We cannot assign God a definite form and say that God is precisely this or that.
What we call Brahman is the same as God.
Brahman means the Greatest, the Absolute—the eternal Being
that suffuses all known space and beyond.

Today scientists say that the universe is egg-shaped.
For thousands of years in India, the universe was referred to
as Brahmandam, the Great Egg.

The Shiva Linga is a microcosm of the vast cosmic Egg.
It refers to the cosmos as the positive form of divine Consciousness.
The word *Shiva* means *auspicious,* referring to unqualified, formless, absolute Reality,
the source and support of all Existence.
For the ancient seers the Shiva Linga symbolized the first stage between Brahman,
the Absolute, and the manifest Universe.

Linga does not mean *phallus* — not even a fool
would pray to the male sex organ for protection.

God is not a personage seated on a ceremonial throne somewhere above the sky.
It is way beyond the reach of human intellect — It is pure Experience.
God cannot be seen with our physical eyes —
only by gazing within can we experience God.

Human beings are the children of the universe
and have the opportunity to be reborn as the children of God.
When we die to the ego and its final traces fade away —

not when we are dying but while we are still alive—
is when our true identity as the Supreme Self is born.

Strive to reach that state in which everything is known to be part of your Self.

The basic requirements for liberation are continuous remembrance of God
and Love for all sentient and insentient being.
When your heart becomes that expansive,
freedom is only a step or two away.

Self-realization is nothing but the ability—
the openness of heart—to love equally all that is.

Three manifestations of Love awaken within us:
First Love for oneself,
then Love for the Divine
and finally Love for all Creation.

We can only develop the ability and the power to recognize God in all things
when we can see God in ourselves.
Once we realize our own godliness we are able to see it in others.
We can see God, the Uninvited, everywhere.

Love for oneself does not mean the self-centered love of the ego,
but the Love of life that affirms our own divinity
and acknowledges both success and failure as divine blessings.
Love for oneself matures into Love for God
and together they generate Love for Creation.

Eventually, the real seeker of Truth uncovers the Soul's eternal unity
with everything observable.
Identifying with indivisible Existence
we merge—in ineffable exultation and rapture—
as duality gives way to the One.

Happiness and unhappiness belong to the world.
God is the Bliss beyond all duality.

God is like infinite Sunlight.

Children, we are the light of God—
the eternally free, infinite and blissful Supreme Self.
Proceed with innocence, effort and faith, and you will discover
the bliss of the Self within you.

Whenever you feel inspired and have time, sit in solitude
and try to visualize everything as pure Light and bliss Consciousness.

Pray to merge in the supreme Soul and grace will fill you with supreme Power.

Once the dam of ignorance breaks, you will enjoy eternal Grace.

Self-realization is the feeling of utter fullness,
of wanting nothing more—the feeling that life is perfect.

Once we know our own true Essence we understand that It is all that exists.

Although things seem to be different, they are all a manifestation of the Self.

One with supreme Consciousness, we are one with all Creation—
we are not only the body but the Life Force that radiates from everything,
making it beautiful and alive.

May the full Moon of Wisdom cause the tides of Love and compassion
to rise high in your hearts!

All great masters have uniquely smiling eyes.
Look at Kali dancing on Shiva's chest!
Though She looks fierce, She has a smile in her eyes—

the blissful smile of Omniscience!
When beholding the bliss of Reality, our eyes are radiant with pure joy.
Like a child looking at the colors of the rainbow,
laughing with wonderment in its eyes,
we begin to laugh with joy.

When we merge into the Self,
the immense vault that holds all the secrets of the Cosmos
opens before us and we see our Self in everything.
We are pure enough to love and serve all—
which is humanity's highest goal.

Finding your Self and loving everything equally are basically the same thing.

We are Love Itself.

Nothing but Love should ever flow from us toward others.

Once we feel I am not the master but the servant,
we become gods and goddesses in the realm of Love.

Through the innocence, purity and Love born of Self-knowledge,
may Mother's children rise and waken to the Infinite.

May my children be able to see everything in themselves and themselves in everything.

Life is a great journey from Consciousness to Consciousness.

The real meaning of I is pure Consciousness.

Never forget, your real source is Supreme Being.

Never forget your true home.

Children, Mother's Love will never run dry.
It is not given intentionally—It overflows.

Mother does not do anything.
Pure Being, doing nothing, does everything.

Love simply overflows....

20

THE FLOWER

Everything belongs to the Universe.

How can we speak of ownership when nothing belongs to us?
This world is a temporary stop—
we are only here as visitors.

Life is a rented room in a lodge that will be inhabited by many others after us.

There is a Power beyond all this.
The body is a temporary dwelling.
Our permanent home is the Soul.

Many of us believe that individual life begins and ends at some fixed time.
But in reality, Life is a flowing, ever-changing river that has no beginning or end.
From the riverbank we only only see a short stretch of the river—
we cannot see its source or its outlet.

Our minds do not have the capacity to measure and know the river's length or depth—
that is God's mystery.
Our minds are only a finite collection of fragmented thoughts and feelings
but God is one and infinite.

What is imperfect cannot grasp perfection.

When we watch a puppet show we forget everything else,
temporarily believing that the puppets are moving and dancing by themselves—
when actually invisible hands move them behind a screen.
A supreme Power acts behind Creation.

Birth and death are only relative
and from the ultimate point of view they are unreal.

When we say that the external world is not real but illusory,
we do not mean that it does not exist
but that it is impermanent and constantly in flux.

Death may destroy the body at any time or place,
but in the realm of Soul nothing changes—the soul is never destroyed.

With every birthday we take another step closer to Death.
Our birthday is also a death-day.

Death is always stalking us like a shadow.

Death has been tracking us since our birth.
Before it catches us, we have so much to accomplish.
We must prepare to leave this temporary body at any moment.
We need to ask ourselves why we are on this journey, what is our goal
and whether we are on the right path or lost.

One day Death will snatch everything.
We will not be able to keep our precious bodies, or even a pin.
Accept this profound truth and surrender yourself at the feet of the Supreme.
Be happy and content with whatever comes your way.

The instincts of life and Love reverberate in every creature.
No one wants to die—everyone wants to live and live and live!
We will cling to anything, even if it costs us the universe.

Death is the ultimate threat to the ego.
It is the greatest fear and the supreme blow.
To avoid thinking about it, we concentrate on earthly pleasures and indulgences
and strive to satisfy our incessant desires.

There is no greater fear than the fear of Death.

We constantly grasp at worldly pleasures to deny and forget the reality of Death.

We squander our precious mental powers on the insignificant and the impermanent.

While emphasizing our mortal bodies, we neglect our immortal souls.
This has to change!

The ego with all its attachments, anger and fear, destroys all our peace.
We do not realize that in the process of gaining, possessing and mastering,
we are actually losing — we are approaching a huge and irreplaceable loss:
the lost opportunity to free ourselves from the unending cycle of death and rebirth.

Why should we allow a bird of flight to build a nest on our head?

We should not take transitory things so seriously!

The basic problem is our confusion over what is permanent
and what is impermanent.

The true Self is the only thing that lasts.

Though ocean waves rise and fall in myriad shapes, they are always water.
A realized Soul understands that death is a natural change that the body must undergo
in the journey from birth to death—and thus feels no fear.
Ordinary people who identify with the body experience themselves as a single wave.
Anticipating that they will disappear forever, they fear the failure of the body
and try to avoid death.

Only if we identify with the body, do we die.
An egoless person cannot die
because he or she is no longer a body but Consciousness itself.

Remember, your present life is only an infinitesimal portion of your total life.
Your existence does not end after only one life.

God has given us an aura with unlimited infinite energy
that can be charged to any degree.
We can travel in any world, even in a world devoid of air.
Death can be transcended.
You are never born and you never die.
Your soul exists forever.
Do not fear death, and do not worry about your next birth.

The soul is not born, nor does it die.
The concept of birth should be abandoned altogether!

Where do we go when we die?
Nowhere.

When the light bulb burns out, the electricity remains.

When the body dies, pure Being remains.

Death is only a period — a pause — between two sentences.
The period is placed at the end of the sentence so a new sentence may begin.

Although the eagle causes the leaves to fall, they are ready to fall.
The individual soul leaves the body, but the supreme Soul is eternal.

There are no mistakes about the time of death.

Children, learn to accept and welcome Death.
Be friendly to Death, and Death will become your friend.
Once we learn to accept Death, many of our fears will disappear
and we will be able to live in peace.

The awareness that death can happen at any moment
helps us to develop real faith and come closer to God.

Growing old is a journey toward Death.
Growing up is a journey toward Immortality.

Only when we understand the inevitability of death
do we experience the urgency to seek inner peace and true happiness.

Constant remembrance of the possibility of death is the best way to learn humility.

The next moment does not belong to us—only the present.
Living in the present, dropping the past, forgetting the future—this is real living.
We do not know whether we will be here, in this body, one second from now.

Great saints and sages always live in the present moment.

We cannot know Death without knowing life.
For those who have known life, Death is the flower of life.
That is why the great masters, in spite of their physical pain, smile blissfully at Death.

Having embraced all their life experiences, good and bad, with great Love,
they can embrace Death in the same way.

Death is the flowering of life.

Once we are thankful for everything, we can give it up with a wonderful smile.
We can lovingly embrace Death in its extreme beauty
not as a frightening enemy, but as our dearest friend.

To open ourselves to the experience of death, we must be fearless and wide-awake.
If we are afraid, we will be closed.
It takes great depth, fearlessness, awareness and wakefulness
to consciously experience the bliss of death.

If we can transcend our attachment to this body and mind,
death is not only painless, it is as blissful as leaping into a pool of water.

In both birth and death, we are utterly helpless.
The ego recedes into the distant background.
During and after death, we are normally unconscious of what is happening.
Because of the intensity of both birth and death,
Nature has arranged for us to forget these major moments.

After our death, our longing to know the supreme Truth floats like a bubble
in the subtle aura that carries our individual tendencies into our next body.

If we can remain conscious and alert as we pass through death and birth,
they are only another experience and do not disturb us.
We are able to smile — but this only happens
when we are merged with the Source.

At death, some Souls rise like helium balloons and burst and merge with everything.
Others, due to their good deeds and karma, rise upward
and later return to play out their remaining karma.
Still others do not rise at all — their habits and attachments bind them
as if to a rock — and they are reborn.

If we die in a state of extremely profound meditation, we will not be reborn.

If we wish for world peace at our death or feel deep love for Amma,
we will be with Her when She takes another incarnation.
If we can imagine infinite Light and embrace It, we will be liberated.
But this takes lifelong practice and has to be deeply rooted in our heart and being.

Our next life is determined by our last thought.
Whatever we are really attached to will determine our final thought.

The final thought is determined by the habits that we have cultivated.
Actions become our habits and habits become our personality,
and so they consume us — we become what we do.

Our character is created by our habits.
We should constantly bear in mind that our final thought
will reflect the characteristics we have cultivated.

We need to prepare for our death.
Whatever your condition, try to keep your mind focused on God.

If you are in pain at the end, morphine is the best option.
If still conscious, you should be allowed to die in peace without pain,
so you can remember God.

Children, if you can chant your mantra incessantly
while leaving your body,
your vital life force will merge into God.

Be conscious of your every movement
and slowly you will awaken fully—even while dying.

Dying is an art, and like any art has to be learned and practiced.
Every time we meditate we are learning to die.

Fear only exists for the ego, and whenever we practice releasing the ego
we are practicing dying.

Many people, though unconscious while dying,
are still struggling helplessly with Death.

Children, do not die unconsciously—learn how to die consciously!
Then you will be able to decide where and what you wish to be in your next life—
or if you want to come back at all.

Real dying is a conscious witnessing of the death of your own body.
As embodiments of Consciousness, we should learn to live and die consciously.

Only the mind of a human being has the capacity to grow to full maturity
and attain immortality—
that is, if the path of spiritual awareness is followed.

Beyond the mind, there is no death and dying.
Once the ego is overcome, death does not exist—we are immortal.

Once we overcome the ego, we are simply an offering to the world.

Children, learn to die blissfully and experience death as a moment of great celebration.

Like other joyful moments in life, death can also be a joyful experience.

Our entire life should be a preparation to die happily.
Only when we are willing to face Death happily, can we live a truly happy life.

Children, remember, this body is only a rental.
One day we will be asked to leave and will have to go.
While still here in a physical body, let us discover the Eternal.

Once we know our permanent home, we will happily leave this rental to enter the house of God.

21
FAITH

All of life rests upon faith.
Every step forward requires faith.

Life is impossible
without faith.

Faith is the union of awareness and Love.
Without it, life cannot go on.

Many people say that faith is blind,
but Amma says that intellect and logic are blind.

Although science has attained heights previously unimaginable,
isn't the universe still a huge mystery?

In spite of all its amazing achievements, science has not yet grasped
even an infinitesimal portion of what the universe really is.

In the modern era, humanity has become hypnotized by the mind.

Why should we place our faith in a mind that jumps from thought to thought
like a monkey leaping from branch to branch?

The tendency of the mind to doubt everything and everyone causes great sorrow.

Without faith in the ultimate Reality, the mind has nothing to hold onto!
We are crippled and paralyzed by fear.

Fear destroys life.
It weakens us and impels us into selfishness and wickedness.
It comes from believing we are weak — from our ignorance
of the cosmic Power within us.
It causes the mind to shrivel up into a tiny dark cell.
We should never become a slave to fear!

Without faith we are afraid,
and our fear damages and disables the mind and the body.
With faith the heart opens to giving and receiving Love.

Ancient Vedic wisdom teaches us to overcome fear
by transforming the belief "I cannot do this" into "only I can do this."
The core of the eternal Way is fearlessness.

Faith and self-confidence are interdependent.

Faith in God fuels faith and confidence in the true Self.
It gives the kind of confidence we need to be truly successful in life.

In every field of life we see people with faith succeeding
and people without it falling by the wayside.

Regardless of whether we believe in Krishna or Christ,
Kali or Mary, a mountain, a flame, a formless God
or an ideal like World Peace —
we need faith!

We need faith in a supreme Power beyond the mind and senses,
that controls the entire Cosmos and drives the intellect.

We do not need to be afraid —
an invisible Hand is always guiding us through life.

Only when we have developed faith in the power behind the Cosmos
are we able to develop a truly discerning intelligence.

Only by recognizing the universal Truth that is God and living in accordance
with its principles, can we enjoy a peaceful journey through life.

We can go through life without believing in a supreme Power,
but to proceed with firm unfaltering steps in a crisis
we must turn to the Truth and follow the Eternal.

Amma is not saying we should believe everything people say,
but that we should have faith in the words of the great sages, saints and souls
who have realized the ultimate goal of life.

Faith in the Supreme Being produces a strong balanced mind
capable of coping with life's most challenging circumstances.

Faith that God is with us gives us the energy and enthusiasm we need
to overcome the numerous obstacles that present themselves along the way.

Faith in the Supreme Being gives us the feeling of security
and protects us from negative forces.

Faith tunes our minds and makes it possible for us to experience
the energy of sacred places.

If we do not have faith in a supreme Power or ideal,
we cannot escape the grips of karma.
Faith gives us immense strength for confronting our fate.
Faith is a strong protective force
that diminishes the effects of the karmic cycle greatly.

Take refuge in the Omnipresent, the Omniscient and the Omnipotent
that is manifest in everything.

Advance with the aim of fully realizing the supreme Reality.
Why wander aimlessly through life?
Avoid delusion.

An invisible Presence informs every moment of our lives.

Everything is God's will and for followers of God, divine grace is incessant.
Compassion incarnate gazes on us with a mercy
far beyond our understanding.

God provides for all those who believe *You are my sole refuge and savior.*
God cures the diseases of those have complete faith and devotion.

Children, even destiny can be altered by sincere dedicated effort
combined with God's grace.

Knowing that we must reap the fruits of our actions,
believers are able to perform practices and good works
that neutralize the negative effects of past wrongs.

The Light of God needs no candles or offerings.
It is we who need to burn candles and make offerings to help us open our hearts.
Since everything belongs to God, what have we to offer anyway?

Let us live in the knowledge that God will protect us,
that everything belongs to God,
that nothing is ours—and God will take care of everything.

Belief and disbelief will always exist—the world exists because of them.
Once our belief is solid, our disbelief will vanish
and we will stop wondering who we are.
If we strive for perfect faith, one day we will know.

Amma does not mean that you should believe in Her
or some God in the sky, but that you should believe in yourself—
everything is within you!

God exists in everyone and everything
and everyone exists in God.

Nothing is needed from the outside—everything is already inside us.

Either follow God's will, understanding "Everything is You."
Or inquire "Who am I," understanding "Everything is within me."

Inquire into the source of the Power within you.
With faith and meditative experience,
you will gain real knowledge of Reality and experience the peace of Oneness.

Any belief acquired through mere telling, hearing or reading will not last,
but belief that comes from actual experience lasts forever.

Have faith in your Self—try to understand who you are and discover your true Self.
Otherwise, even with faith in God, it is very difficult to evolve.

Real faith is faith in your real Self.

Absolute faith is the realization of your true Self.

Turn your gaze away from the world and focus on the Truth that shines within.
Do not look for peace and happiness outside like the musk deer chasing its own scent.

Our main problem is that looking to the outside has become such a habit.

A spiritual seeker must wear blinders like a horse to avoid distraction.

May we develop true faith in ourselves
and stop relying on others for comfort and consolation.
This is the only way that we will ever find true contentment and fulfillment.

Without faith we cannot really feel, be kind or experience Love.

Compassion is born of faith.

To God or a saint, it is immaterial whether we have faith in them or not.
They do not need the faith of others—but we do need their grace
and only through faith can we receive it.

It does not really matter whether we are believers, non-believers or skeptics.
Non-believers who believe in themselves can lead a happy and successful life.
We do not need to believe in Mother or God on a celestial throne—only in ourselves.
Without that, what use would belief in God be anyway?

The point of faith in God is to strengthen our faith and confidence in our Self.
Without our true Self, we will never succeed.
Confidence in our Self gives us the balance, courage and mental control
to confront the inevitable challenges of life.
How can we face them without faith in ourselves?

Faith helps us to control our thoughts and emotions and experience inner harmony.

It is crucial to face life's difficulties with Love and faith.
If we try to run away from our own shadow
we will only collapse in exhaustion.

Life is like a cave we want to explore, but once we get inside
we feel claustrophobic and want to get out.

Self-confidence is like a filter that helps us stay calm
while working on releasing our negativities — so we can continue on our journey.

If we have to proceed slowly because of our old habits, we will need the support
of our faith and confidence to keep purifying ourselves of negative tendencies.

Even when we see darkness all around, we should try to keep moving forward
without becoming depressed and keep the Light burning inside us.

Darkness is simply the absence of Light.

Always remember, when the night comes, it carries the dawn in its womb.
Darkness never lasts forever.
When the time is ripe, the dawn will break.

The wheel of time is always turning.
Fate comes in so many different forms,
and change sometimes comes quickly, sometimes slowly.
Never consider taking your life!
Hold onto prayer.
Hold onto God firmly.

When we are in pain, we must hold onto God very tightly.

Amma is shocked when people come to Her and say they have suffered so much they wish they were dead—these self-pitying thoughts are useless.

We can never foresee when grace will come.
We can only wait — so just relax.

Once you open your heart, you will see
that there was never any darkness, only light.
Even when darkness surrounds you,
remember, it carries the dawn in its womb.

The days will go by whether we laugh or we cry — so why not laugh?

Laughter is a great medicine
and a prophylactic for the disease of seriousness.

Never fall victim to pessimism — let us do what we must and act with optimism.

If we have optimistic faith and put forth effort,
we shall not fail to reach our goal.
But if we are pessimistic, we will descend into even greater darkness and despair,
lose our strength and mental clarity, and feel abandoned and alone.

An unseen Hand is leading us—never lose faith that life will turn around for the better.
Some actions bear immediate fruit, others bear fruit later—
do not worry about your bad actions in a past life.

The past is a cancelled check—it will never return
and tomorrow will never become today.
We have only the present.
We should always act with complete surrender to the Almighty.
This minimizes unpleasantness and helps us to advance.

Optimism is the light of the Self.
It is a form of grace that allows us to be more perceptive
and see life with more clarity.

Never lose your courage, or your faith in God and life!
Always be optimistic, whatever circumstances you face.
This is extremely important!
Pessimism is a form of darkness and ignorance that blocks the Light.
It is a kind of illusory curse created by the illusory mind.

Like a boulder —
it takes a lot of time to raise the mind to a higher level
and only a moment to push it down.

Pessimism and suffering are products of the ego.
Look at the overwhelming optimism of Nature that never stops producing more life.

Patience, optimism, faith and enthusiasm are the keys.
Continue to cultivate these qualities and nourish them in your heart.
Optimism is a very powerful tool for overcoming sorrow.

Smile, care, help others, meditate, and try to remain optimistic!

Life is full of divine Light
but only when we are optimistic can we see it.

We do not belong to the darkness—it is not our home.
We belong to the light—we are the light of God.

When people lose faith in the supreme Reality
there can be no peace or harmony in society.
Without faith people do what they wish—ethics and morality disintegrate
and people behave like instinctual animals.

Without faith, Love, patience and forgiveness—life becomes hell.

Life is a mystery we can only understand when we surrender to it.
Rarely does it turn out as we expected.

We call from the top of the stairs, "I'm coming!"
when we have not the faintest idea what will happen next.

It is crucial to cultivate an attitude of surrender.
Surrender means accepting and welcoming everything
without sadness or disappointment.

We should accept Supreme Being as our only protector and guide.

We should surrender everything to the Supreme and It will protect us.
The Supreme is here and now.

Based on her experience, Amma can assure you that if you surrender fully,
God will make sure you lack for nothing.

The important thing is not how we die but how we live.

Every experience is a guru.
It is often said that life is the great Guru
since it presents us with many lessons and tests.
From our good experiences, we draw inspiration
and from our mistakes, we learn to correct and improve ourselves.

The past is fact—learning from the past and faith in the present
allow us to face the future as a friend.

Always maintain a positive attitude towards life.

Never look backward in grief—always look forward with a smile.

Faith will open your heart and lead you to Love.

People always dream of a good tomorrow—even during sad and painful times
our dreams make life bright and fragrant.

Never give up your hope or your faith.

**Never give up hope!
It is our hope and our belief in a better future
that invigorates us amid the greatest sorrow.**

**Life and God are synonymous.
You are a child of Life, and Life would never close every door.
The infinite Love of God makes such cruelty impossible.
Even if all the doors seem closed, some have been left ajar.
Just knock and they will open.**

**Let us have faith that God is always with us
and this will give us the energy and enthusiasm we need
to overcome all the obstacles.
Never lose hope!**

Never lose contact with the great force of Life.

God is the universal Mind, the unity of Creation.

God or Goddess is always with us
and when we cry with pure longing
will always appear.

Never forget your real Source—never leave your Center.
Even the law of karma turns impotent in the presence of divine Grace.

Always maintain your faith and your fervor.
The spiritual Energy that you have gained from your practices
will always be with you.
Your efforts and their fruits can never be destroyed.
Never, never, never give up hope!

There will always be darkness and light.
That is the very nature of Creation.

Is it not because there is darkness that we know the greatness of Light?

Children, there could be no world without duality.

Without duality there would be no guru or disciple.
How could we contemplate "I am the Self" without the finite mind?
Even in Vedantic reflection, there is duality.

Therefore, do not live in fear.
Cultivate an attitude of acceptance and tell yourself,
"Whatever happens, I will be strong, courageous and happy."

Try to be accepting—the more accepting you are, the more fearless you will be,
and the more fearless you are, the more loving you will be
since you will have no expectations.

Do not think of your life as the result of bad karma
but as the return journey to your Source.

A tenth of what we experience is karma;
the rest is our reaction to it!

Be courageous!—a courageous person never dies,
but a coward is always dying.
Be confident!—confidence boosts us to our destination.
Be decisive! Ask what you can offer.

Strength is the most important quality for the individual and for the nation.
When we become aware of the strength within us, our true Strength awakens.

Break through the wall that separates you from the Supreme Being.
Allow your mind to flow constantly toward the Truth.
Nothing is bad, everything is good—see the Goodness!
Allow your mind to open and pour out its sweetness.

Once we understand the impermanence of the world
and the vulnerability of the ego,
our faith begins to grow.

Once we realize we can die at any moment,
our faith in and longing for God comes alive.

Faith rises up from the heart and pulls us down from the head.
Never let your intellect consume your heart and your faith.

The fountain of Peace springs from the heart not the head.

In a society ruled by selfishness, our greatest treasure is our devotion.
Devotion creates an authentic meeting and union of the individual and universal Self.

Devotion is not blind superstitious belief but a kind of faith
that removes the darkness from our hearts.
Not only does it unburden the heart, it amplifies our sense of what is right
and inspires us with compassion for those who are suffering.

When we lack compassion, it is easy to destroy life.
When we lack concern for others, it means we lack faith in all-encompassing Life.
Compassion is an extension of faith.
Devotion to God and compassion for the world are inseparable —
they are two sides of the same coin.

The real question is not whether God exists, but whether people are suffering.
The devotional path is the practical way to eliminate suffering.
Bhakti is a practical science.

Devotion is not, as some may think, a sign of mental weakness
but rather the triumph of human life.
It means that we can see God in all things equally —

that we have realized the pure Love of selfless Being.

When we say heart, we mean that all the elements of the mind—
memory, ego, intellect and emotion—are functioning together
in the right proportion and at a high level.

Bhakti, devotion, is emotion at a higher level.

The heart is the booster rocket to God.

If knowledge is the fruit of the tree, devotion is the nectar.

Devotion, the Love of selfless Being, is the greatest achievement of all.

When we worship the Eternal through one of the many symbolic instruments,
we are able to feel It all the more clearly and vividly.

When a poet sees a flower she writes a poem.
When a scientist sees it, he studies and researches it.
A young man gives it to a girl.
A worm devours it, and a lover of God offers it to the Beloved.
Everyone's approach is different—everyone has the right to accept or reject it.
For Amma, all approaches are valid.
People have all kinds of reactions—this is the way of the world.
We have the right to believe or not to believe.
Amma's approach is what can She do that is positive?

Faith, devotion and conscious action are the teachings of the Eternal Way.

Amma's only desire is to worship and serve.
Each of us understands things from our own perspective.
A poet seeing a flower composes a poem—and someone else offers it to God.
A maggot consumes it and a scientist studies it.
Regardless of what people say, Amma focuses on what She can do.

Some people think that God is nothing more than a belief.
In reality, God exists in the human heart.

God's only eyes, hands and legs are our own.

Look into the eyes of a child and you will see God.

God is the cosmic Power within us.

To say we do not believe in God is like saying
we do not have a tongue—when we are speaking with it!

As with the giant tree that arises from a seed—
divine Power drives the entire universe.

Shelter in all-knowing, ever-present, all-powerful God
manifested in everything that exists.
Go forward with the single-minded aim of realizing the ultimate Reality.

Why wander aimlessly?
Avoid delusions that veil the true meaning of life.

We worship God to nurture our own divinity.
If we can develop divine qualities without faith, there is no need for it.
But whether we recognize and acknowledge God or not,
the great One—untouched by our inability to recognize It—
remains the undiminished Truth.

God, the Supreme Being, is the only Truth.
Only when we realize this, will our lives be complete.
Only then, will we taste the nectar of Immortality.

Child, never lose your courage, or your faith in God and life.
Always be optimistic, regardless of the circumstances.
With faith and courage, anything can be accomplished!

Be brave as a lion—while your heart is melting like butter.

It takes faith and effort to reach the other shore.

Absolute faith is the realization of God.

Repeat your mantra, do good deeds, pray for divine grace
and everything you need will be given.

Patience, enthusiasm and optimism—may these three be the mantras of our lives.

As you shoulder your responsibilities, never forget to smile.

The smile that blossoms on your lips is the signature of God.
Never lose your smile or your faith in God.

True knowledge and right attitude help us more than anything
to face life's ups and downs.

Remember, "God is with me — I have the power to do anything!"

Faith can create a flow so powerful that it engulfs the whole universe!

We have the choice to make life happy or unhappy.

Come what may, never let go of your happiness.

If we decide to, we can create an Empire of Happiness — for that is our real nature.
The light of happiness burns in every heart —
never close the drapes of desire and block its radiance.

The Sun of Love is always blazing.

If we shut the doors and windows of our house,
how will we experience the light of God's Love?
Open the door of your ego—
come out and find the sweetness and coolness of God's Love.

Whatever happens, it is up to each of us to be happy.

Let us make a firm decision to be happy and strong.

Happiness is a decision like any other.
Whether we laugh or we cry, the days go by.
Let us try to smile and be cheerful, engage in good actions,
express kindness in our words and compassion in our glances.
Amma prays to the Supreme Being
that her children may have all the strength they need.
May divine grace protect us always.

Let us realize that our own worries and sorrows are lighter than many others'
and try to be happy with what we have.

Contentment is our greatest treasure.
Always try to be content with what you have.
A compassionate person feels and expresses gratitude.

Gratitude not greed, is the way.

Let us always remember to thank God for blessing us
with a skillful working mind and body,
the chairs and rocks for giving us a place to sit and rest,
Mother Earth for offering us her lap to run, jump and play upon,
the birds for singing, the flowers for blooming, the trees for shading
and the streams for flowing.
Should we not be grateful to everyone and everything?

Gratitude is our inner connection to God, to Creation and to humanity.

Let us not allow the dark clouds of selfishness to obscure
the beautiful moonlight of gratitude.

Be thankful! It is the best way to be released
from the physical and mental confinement of the mind and body
into the vast expanse of the inner life.

Thankfulness is the humble, open, prayerful attitude
that allows us to receive more of God's grace.

When our minds are full of thanks we are spontaneously happy.

It is not joy that brings us thankfulness, but thankfulness that brings us joy.

The truly wealthy smile even in the face of great suffering and death.

Death can happen at any time or place—like the period at the end of a sentence followed by another sentence—one life leads to the next.

Death is an inevitable part of life that everyone must face, either today or tomorrow.

Let us leave our bodies laughing!

Our divine radiant Essence can never be destroyed.

If we have optimistic faith and put forth effort, we cannot fail to reach the goal.

Do not cry, my darling child—Mother is always with you.

Have faith, my children, and have no fear—
Mother is with you.

22

THE BEAUTY OF LIFE

**Isn't Beauty
the very nature of God?**

God gives life its beauty and makes life what it is.

**God is the Beauty of all beauty—
the beauty, purity and harmony behind everything
down to the slightest detail.**

**The vast pattern of beauty and order that pervades Creation
reveals a prodigious heart and intelligence.**

How could such perfect beauty and order exist without a cosmic Intelligence
and Power arranging everything?

Supreme Being manifests through our actions as goodness,
through our minds as truth
and through our hearts as beauty.

The beautiful melody of a flute is not to be found in the flute
or the player's hands, or even in the composer's heart.
It originates beyond the finite—in the supreme Consciousness
experienced by the soul.

Music comes from a realm that transcends body and mind—
it comes from pure Consciousness.

Art is divine Beauty revealed to us through its many splendid forms,
such as painting, music, dance and sculpture.

Music, poetry, painting and sculpture are all expressions of the heart of their creator.

Creativity is a power that comes from beyond,
which we experience within.
Each of us uses this power in a special way,
but it is always the same power.

People display all kinds of talents outwardly,
but they all arise from the same Source.
Ink can be used to write or to draw, as long we will become the pen
and allow the ink to flow.

When we pour our hearts and souls into any activity,
it can become a source of great inspiration.

When a singer sings from her heart,
she is touched with divinity!

Art is one of the easiest ways to realize our innate divinity.

Artists pour themselves into their work and then they vanish—
leaving only their music or poetry—
leaving their Love.

It is the artist's Love
that gives great works of art their extraordinary beauty.

For a poet, words are Love.

Art depends upon Love.

Love is the ambrosia that saturates life with beauty and magic.

Anything made with Love has a palpable luminosity, vitality and magnetism.

In Love there is always beauty.
Everyone is unique
and in every heart there is Love.
Let us try to put Love into everything we do.

Mother—the power of Creation—is within us.

When our creative efforts are founded on Love and compassion for the world—
that is when they become truly valuable.

Love banishes all fear and transforms all ugliness into beauty.

Ugliness is the first step on the path to Beauty.

Before a sculptor begins to sculpt, he has to face the rough stone.

To understand and appreciate beauty, we need to be able to recognize ugliness.

Pain is an excellent fertilizer for producing flowers of goodness and beauty.

Only when we are strong enough to bear suffering
can we transform ugliness into beauty.

Beauty—like peace—is only found within.

Beauty is born from our innermost, heart-felt faith.

For Amma, there is beauty in everyone.
She is always stunned by the splendor She beholds in everyone.

The lotus flowers in the mud, but a pure mind sees only the beauty of the flower.

What makes God's Creation seem ugly is primarily the mind.

The ego is a cataract that prevents us from enjoying the beauty of the world.

It is difficult to let go of the ego—and ultimately only divine grace can remove it.
But by fondling a bubble that can burst at any moment
we risk losing the eternal beauty of God.

The secret of beauty lies in unity and equality.
When we join in the diversity of life, we experience its beauty.

This world of flowers, oceans, skies, birds, forests, mountains and valleys
is so beautiful—God made this earth beautiful!
May we see and love the divine Beauty
that pervades everything.

The world is a vast floral garden in a myriad shades and scents.

May divine Beauty pervade each and every life
and all our hearts be unified in a glorious garden of Beauty.

When our hearts finally open to all,
society will blossom in splendor and beauty.

Human beings who live in service to Life are the real beauty of society.

If only one tree grows in the desert, there is shade.
If only one flower blossoms, there is beauty.

Once we realize that birth and death are neither the beginning nor the end,
our lives will become infinitely beautiful and blissful.

If we live our life in beauty, it will culminate in a beautiful death.

Pour yourself into everything you do and you will experience beauty and Love.

They are within you—express them in all your actions
and you will touch the very source of bliss.

Beauty, beauty, beauty everywhere!
Yes, there is ugliness too—try to transform it into beauty
and your soul will be happy.

If you can beautify your prison cell, you may even find the key to escaping it!

God gave to the lightening and rainbow only a few moments to live,
to the butterfly a few days, to certain flowers one day
and to the full moon only until dawn.
But these brief lives give us so much beauty and delight!
Amma prays that, learning from their example, we will use our lives
to make the world more and more beautiful.

Freedom from sorrow is not something we achieve after death, in some other world.

It is realized in this world while we are still alive.
This is the principle Lord Krishna taught with the example of his life—
which celebrated all of life, even its failures, with gusto.
Instead of making others cry, let us live to make others smile.

The most beautiful smile in the world
is the smile that lights a face brimming over with Love.

When our minds are completely open,
we can experience the pure sweet beauty of Love.

The light of Love is the essence of true Beauty.

Love is the beauty of Life.

23
THIS MOMENT

Only this moment is real.

Moment by moment life vanishes
like water dripping through a cracked cup.

Our most precious treasure is time.
Anything lost can be found again except time.
We should live every moment in the conscious awareness that,
with every tick of the clock, Death takes one step closer.

The world is only a temporary stop on a journey.
We are here for only a short while.
Yet we keep racing after money and things
as if we will live forever.

There is no way to make sure we are safe and secure
because the next moment is not in our hands.
Only the present moment is ours.

Everything is in flux.
Death can occur at any moment.
Take every moment as it comes.
Approach life without any expectations or fixed ideas.

Only this moment is ours—in the next we may die.
Only this moment is guaranteed,
so live it consciously and beautifully.

The things of this world are fragile and at any moment may disappear.
Even the next breath is not under our control.
This is why it is so important to live every moment with awareness and joy.

Dwelling on the past is like embracing a corpse.
Dwelling on the future is like trying to sleep by the den of a cobra.

This moment is all we have!
If we spend it lamenting over the past and worrying about the future,
we miss its beauty altogether.
If we live it wisely, the future will brighten.

Whenever we worry, we use our imagination
to materialize what we do not want.

Only when we live in the present
and act wholeheartedly, do actions bear fruit.

When we worry, we do not make our best effort
and thwart the desired result.

The past is like a cancelled check—it will never come back!
Tomorrow will never become today.
We have only the present.

Time measures our lives and memories,
allowing us to think about childhood, aging and death.
But in reality, nothing exists but the present.
The future is a question for which there is no answer.
Focus on the present, nurture the seed, and the tree will grow.

All our actions bear fruit: The future is the fruit.
Do not worry about the future—be patient.
Focus on the moment.
Act with consciousness and Love.

Out of this moment comes the next.

The present moment is the cause
of our happiness in the next.

Try to forget what you cannot find
and find in the present what you need.

Desire is in the mind—the soul is beyond the mind.
It is the desireless stillness within.
The soul is always a happy child.

Once you free yourself from all your thoughts of the past,
your heart will spontaneously fill with peace.

Allow your memories to bring back positive feelings.
Remember the positive things that people have done—

the encouragement and support they have given you.
Draw energy from the past for your life in the present.

No matter how powerful the past, how we deal with the present
is much more important —
for it is what determines the future.

Great saints and sages always live in the present.

Amma only lives in the present — so how can there ever be death?

For Mother the present is far more important
than what has to be done tomorrow.
Mother does not worry about the next moment.
Love, joy, being and enlightenment — all take place in the present.

The next moment is not ours — only this one belongs to us.

Living in the present,
dropping the past and forgetting the future—
that is real living.

Remembering God is the best medicine
for forgetting the past
and also avoiding anxiety about the future.

Renunciation means renouncing both past and future.
The past is a garbage bin where we dump all our actions, good and bad.
The past is a wound we should not touch but allow to heal.
This can happen only if we trust in God.

It is not wrong to make plans.
To build a bridge, we need to make drawings and reflect on them.
But if all we do is plan, we will never get anywhere—
we will only be living in a drawing.
Plan for the future with focused attention, live well in the present,
and beyond that, surrender to the Almighty.

In every action, remember your true Self.

To focus on the Self means to be fully and absolutely in the present,
unaware of the past and the future.
This alone is real prayer.

Every moment of life is a rare and precious opportunity
that should not be wasted.

Every moment, everything is changing.
Change is the very nature of life.
Every day, good and bad happen without warning.
Life is a game whose outcome is unknown to the very end.
Conditions are ever shifting and the players have to pay close attention to every move,
since the slightest lapse in attention can lead to failure.

Every moment is like an examination.

Cultivate awareness in every action!
Concentrate intensely, as if walking on a tightrope over a river.

We do not know whether we will be here, in this body, one second longer.

We should be very careful about everything we say and do,
and should not utter meaningless words or idle away precious time.

There are constant obstacles on the road to Self-realization.
Unless we are very careful, we can easily slip and fall
and wind up wasting our whole life.

Children, we should give our full undivided attention to every word we say,
every step we take and every action we perform.
This is lesson number one.

It is not enough to start doing spiritual practices
when we are in intensive care or lying on our deathbed.
This moment is precious—do not waste it!

Death, the most humbling of all experiences, is always just one step behind us.
Never say tomorrow—now is the time to do whatever is needed.

All our thoughts and actions are recorded on a subtle sheath
that surrounds us and reflects our true growth.
Eventually, the recording will be played back
and determine our next life.

We should always give our full attention to everything we do.
This is the only way to experience the Consciousness
that leads to full realization of the Self.

The effect of doing spiritual practice is to direct the wandering mind
to a single point and make it subtle and powerful.
Without achieving this state of concentration,
Self realization is impossible.

Life is so precious—every moment is priceless.

Love exists in the present, and so does happiness.
God exists in the present, and so does enlightenment.

Do not waste your life acting mechanically.

Children, do not waste a single second!

Life exists only in the present.

The present is our only treasure.
Be alert and aware, and make the best possible use of this moment.

It is crucial to make each moment meaningful.
Sprout new shoots, produce lovely flowers
and offer the succulent fruit of your joy.

Because of our karmas and desires,
we experience both happiness and sorrow in life.
Only with an attitude of acceptance, can we live and progress in peace.

Surrender to the present.

Alive to the present,
we can accept life's circumstances more cheerfully.

Since only this moment belongs to us,
let us be happy now.

**Perform all your actions with joy!
Take pleasure in your work.**

**The present is action, so love every action
and perform it with utmost joy.**

**May your life be a series of festive moments
enjoyed willingly and enthusiastically.**

**Be joyful and alert.
Smile and be kind.**

**As a child is fully present, be present to Love.
Love with your whole being, without reservation.
Do nothing partially.
Do everything fully present in the moment.**

Live in the present moment and make the most of it.

The present moment is *all, all, all* that we have.
Be exceedingly careful not to lose it to sorrow and unhappiness.

Few know the joy and bliss of the present moment.
This moment is everything!
Old ideas are utterly irrelevant.

Every moment is precious
because with each small act of Love and kindness
a new creation is being born.

All our actions should bring joy and happiness to others.
When we share our happiness with others,
our own happiness is multiplied.

Our time here is so limited — let us be like the butterfly
that lives only a few days
and spreads happiness every moment.

Mother does what She does not in order to attain some future result
but for the pure joy of giving Love now.

Be happy and spread happiness!
Let your hearts flower in unison and create a splendid garden.
And if that garden should not materialize,
at least you will have enjoyed a beautiful dream.

May our lives be a burst of laughter from the heart.
That is real religion, real spirituality and real prayer.

Laughter is the music of the soul.

May we be able to laugh at ourselves and weep for others.

Opening our hearts with smiles and laughter, we approach pure Being more closely.

It makes Mother so happy to see her children dancing!

If everyone were happy, would that not be the World's Greatest Wonder?

Experience and create joy!

When we see everything as God, every moment is a miracle.

There is no miracle greater than God.

Every experience is a blessing.

The choice to make our lives happy or unhappy rests in our hands.

Enjoy this moment.

24
PURE LOVE

In the end, the only medicine
that can heal all the wounds of the world is Love.

Love can accomplish anything—
cure disease, heal a broken heart, and transform the human mind.

Love is the divine medicine and the only medicine
that can cure the disease of the ego.

When we experience pure Love,
we are able to overcome the body, the mind, and even fear itself.

Love banishes fear.

There is no obstacle that Love cannot overcome.

For Love, barriers and limits do not exist.

There is no greater power than Love—it is infinite!
Love transcends all material limitations and mental reservations.

Love is Energy in its purest form.
Not an emotion, it is a boundless flow of Power and Consciousness.

An emotion has a particular vibration—it generates
particular waves with particular effects.
Waves of laughter differ from those of anger.

Waves of maternal love differ from those of lust.
But the most powerful waves of all are the waves of pure Love—
which are beyond any comparison.

The energy of Love cannot be conveyed by words.

Pure Love is a constant, uninterrupted, unbreakable flow.

Love embraces and permeates everything with the oneness of Being—
the constant powerful presence of Life itself.

Life and Love are not two, but one.
They are inseparable as a word and its meaning.

Love connects everything in Creation.

Love sustains all of Existence.

Love is the foundation, the beauty and the fulfillment of life.

Love is the pillar that holds up the family, society and Nature.

Love holds the entire universe together.

Love's sole desire is to help, serve and uplift.

Love eliminates negativity.

Love cleanses, purifies and elevates.

Love is the timeless guiding Light
that raises the human mind from the lowest level of emotion
to the highest level of Being.

Love is the very heart of Nature and Life.

Love gives Life its sweetness and meaning.

Love is the breath of the Soul.

Hidden behind everything is Love.

Love is the power, the energy and the inspiration behind every word and action.

Nothing can happen without the power of Love.

The only power that can attract the attention of God is Love.

There is no greater power of attraction than Love.

Love is a magnificent flower of irresistible fragrance.

Love is the springtime of life.
Love rejuvenates and enriches life.

When we truly love, all burdens, problems, conflicts, hostilities,
tensions and fears fade.

Real Love is simply the mind emptied of all fears
and the Self stripped of all masks.

When we love, the intellect empties of all thought,
the mind vanishes and nothing remains but pure innocent Love.

Where there is innocent Love, there is no ego.

Pure Love reveals the Self as it truly is.

Once we experience pure Love, we do not need Love from anyone.
We realize that we are Love, the inexhaustible Source
that constantly supplies Love to all.

Once we know we are embodiments of Love,
we do not need to go searching for peace—peace comes searching for us.
All conflict evaporates like mist in the dawn.

Love alone brings peace and joy.

Love is absolute faith and surrender.

Pure Love allows us to experience complete interior absorption
and true willingness to sacrifice ourselves.

Love involves tremendous sacrifice and sometimes great pain
but always culminates in eternal Bliss.

Love is the constant giving up of everything that is ours.
Yet what is really ours? Only the ego.
Love destroys selfishness.

When Love awakens, the ego dies and divinity is born.
Everything becomes part of our Self.

When we are full of Love we can see God in everything
and that is the ultimate Realization.

All preconceived notions, prejudices and judgments—
all phenomena that stem from the ego—
are consumed in the flames of Love.

Children, when we experience Love, we experience Truth.
Love is Truth, Love is God, Love is Duty.
Love is Bliss beyond bliss.

When we truly love we cannot tell a lie because Truth is all there is.

Love is the divine Truth.

Love is true Knowledge.

Love is Knowledge, Freedom and Bliss.

To be happy in this world, we must have Love and Knowledge.

Love is the gift that makes the giver happier than the receiver.

Love is the direct expression of God.

Children, divine Love is our very nature—it radiates from everyone!

Love is the face of God.

Love is the living manifestation of God.

Love is God's form revealed.

God dwells deep in our hearts as pure and innocent Love.

Love is our true wealth—the fabulous wealth
we still do not realize we possess.

Love is the treasure we should store in our hearts.

Let us fill our hearts with more and more and more Love!
Let us express Love in everything we say and do.

Let us fill our hearts with the light of Love for Divine Being,
for every soul in Creation, and make this world heaven.

If there is a paradise on Earth and in the human heart
it is here—here!—and only here.

May the Tree of each life be deeply rooted in Love.
May all our thoughts, words and actions rise only from Love.
May we all become lamps of Love lighting the world.

Try to become Love.

Let us empower Love within us.

Love is pure Consciousness and does not force — it simply is.
We only need to awaken its Energy within us.

Love is our nature — our unchanging Essence.

Love is always with us as the indestructible light of our own Being.

Love is wholeness and oneness with no other —
no *you* or *I*, no duality or difference.
Love encompasses everything.
Pure, undivided, unending, all-pervasive Love embraces the entire Cosmos.

Love is the one thing that pervades absolutely everything.

We are born in Love, we live our lives in Love and finally we merge in Love.

Spirituality begins and ends with Love—
like a pebble, dropped in a pond, rippling in concentric circles to the shore
and returning to the center.

The selfless giving of Love is a circle without beginning or end.

In everyone there is a boundless spring of Love, and when we tap into it
divine Energy gushes up and floods our hearts.
When our hearts overflow—that is Love!

Love is like water from a spring that never runs dry
no matter how much we take.
The more Love we give, the more Love pours out.

Love begins within us and when it is purified, encircles the entire globe.

In truth, there is no end to Love.

Love's footprints are imprinted forever in the path of time.

Love is eternal.

Love is indestructible.

Love is what keeps the world in balance.
Let us always act from the center of Love.

Love is God.

Love is the God to worship and realize.

Love is the easiest and most natural way to realize Divinity.

Love can transform the individual into God.

Love is the only religion that will ever lift humanity to great and glorious heights.
All religions and philosophies should be strung on a single cord of Love.

Love is the universal language of the heart—the only language
that every creature understands.

Love is the universal religion—
the religion that humanity really needs.

Love is the answer.

Love is the way.

Let Love be your guide.

Love is my religion.

JANINE CANAN MD, **psychiatrist and poet, graduate of Stanford University *with distinction* and New York University School of Medicine, has followed Mata Amritanandamayi for three decades and authored many books of poetry, translations, anthologies, stories and essays, including compilations of Amma's teachings—the award-winning *Messages from Amma: In the Language of the Heart, Garland of Love,* and *Love Is My Religion.***

PRAISES FOR AMMA

"God's Love in a human body." — CONSERVATIONIST JANE GOODALL

"A supernova of spirituality!" — *HINDUISM TODAY*

"Like a Mother, Amma loves unconditionally and serves expediently."
— COMEDIAN RUSSELL BRAND

"Amma has done more than many governments have done for their people."
— NOBEL PEACE LAUREATE MUHAMMAD YUNUS

"Truly a saint." — UNITED NATIONS PARTNERSHIPS

"This celestial being who walks among us!" — AUTHOR WAYNE DYER

"The darkness cannot compete with Her." — ACTOR JIM CARREY

"The embodiment of pure Love — Ammachi heals." — AUTHOR DEEPAK CHOPRA MD

www.ingramcontent.com/pod-product-compliance
Lightning Source LLC
Chambersburg PA
CBHW070530090426
42735CB00013B/2926

9781680378719